RAILWAYS
of
NEW BRUNSWICK

A HISTORY

DAN SOUCOUP

Nimbus Publishing Limited
3731 Mackintosh St, Halifax, NS B3K 5A5
(902) 455-4286 nimbus.ca

Printed and bound in Canada
Cover and interior design: Heather Bryan

Library and Archives Canada Cataloguing in Publication

Soucoup, Dan, 1949-
Railways of New Brunswick : a history / Dan Soucoup.
Includes bibliographical references.
ISBN 978-1-894420-35-8

1. Railroads—New Brunswick—History. I. Title.

HE2809.N3S68 2010   385.09715'1   C2010-904351-0

We acknowledge the financial support of the Government of Canada
through the Book Publishing Industry Development Program (BPIDP) and the
Canada Council, and of the Province of Nova Scotia through the
Department of Tourism, Culture and Heritage for our publishing activities.

CONTENTS

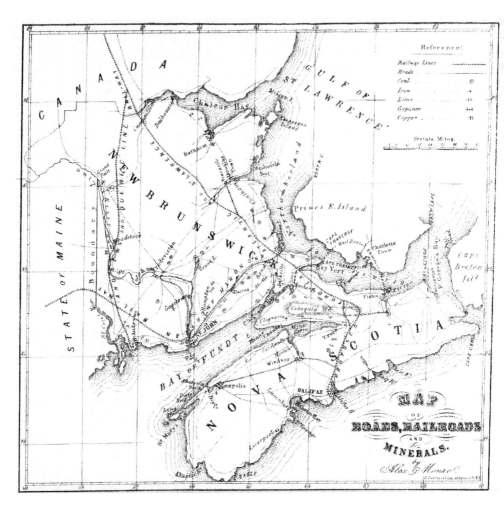

Map of Proposed Roads and Railroads, New Brunswick & Nova Scotia, 1855

PREFACE

HISTORIAN AND SURVEYOR ALEXANDER MONRO of Baie Verte produced an interesting book of New Brunswick. The book was published in 1855 and called *New Brunswick, With a Brief Outline of Nova Scotia and Prince Edward Island, Their History, Civil Divisions, Geography, and Productions.* Monro also produced the enclosed map that is fascinating to look at today especially the railway lines because in the 1850s, so little tracks had been laid and most of the rail lines drawn on this map were only proposed lines. So how accurate was Monro in 1855 predicting where railways would be built? New Brunswick's first railway, the St. Andrews and Quebec Railway is shown heading north to Woodstock and then northeast to connect near Campbellton with the Intercolonial Railway (then called European, Atlantic, and St. Lawrence Railway.) That was not to be since the St. Andrews and Quebec Railway stopped in 1862 in a field outside Woodstock, and while it went into bankruptcy, a line did eventually head north from Woodstock to Edmundston, and on to Quebec. The Western Extension Railway from Saint John to the Maine border did end up crossing over into Maine at McAdam-Vaneboro but first headed north out of Fairville to Fredericton Junction before heading west to McAdam. And the Saint John to Fredericton route along the St. John River would not be built until after the First World War because in the 1860s, the Fredericton Branch Railway had been built to Fredericton Junction to connect with the Western extension Railway. And the Intercolonial Railway—then called the European, Atlantic, and St. Lawrence Railway, is shown coming from Nova Scotia east of Amherst and then heading north to Shediac before bearing northwest to the Miramichi and Campbellton. Dorchester ICR railway commissioner Edward Baron Chandler would make sure the ICR passed through his community and that meant building tracks from Amherst through to Moncton and straight north to the Miramichi.

Introduction

IF HISTORIANS ARE ACCURATE IN ASSERTING that the railway made Canada—building the first transcontinental railway across the northwest to the Pacific assured the growth and prosperity of Confederation—then the same can be said about the railway's affect on New Brunswick. The coming of the railway remade the province in a remarkable new way, replacing the stagecoach and relegated sail power to a secondary role while opening up the interior of the province to new settlement and business opportunities. New Brunswick began building railways in earnest in the 1850s and within two decades, the province was no longer simply a coastal region but had railways and spur lines going off in all directions. The building boom lasting approximately five decades and the downside of the railway expansion was financial turmoil. Most New Brunswick railways were built or supported by government subsidies and lacked a strong business case. Local politicians, schemers, slick promoters, and even some genuine entrepreneurs all were struck by railway fever. Since a subsidy of up to $10,000 per mile usually spurred railway companies to break ground and begin to build their dream railway, the question of whether there would be enough freight or passengers to pay the freight later on was usually not discussed extensively prior to construction. Construction costs on some railways did not even exceed the government subsidy and made money before opening.

In some cases, fly-by-night railway promoters made some money and left the province in a hurry after shoddy construction techniques were revealed. But most railways built before World War I were semi-public works, a kind of public-local private partnership whereby public funds would kick start construction with the hope that once the line opened, enough business would warrant the railway remaining viable. And in general, there wasn't enough business and many railways struggled until being gobbled up by either the Intercolonial or Canadian Pacific. By the late 1920s, most railways in the province belonged to one of these two national railway systems. 1876 was a special year in the history of the railway in eastern Canada. The revolutionary railway age officially began in Maritime Canada. On July 6, the first train ran along the Intercolonial Railway from Halifax to Rivière-du-Loup, linking the east coast with the once remote inland centres of British North America. Yet the same year marked an ending of sorts, one that signalled the closure of an older, more prosperous era. One of New Brunswick's great lumber exporting firms, the Rankin Company, officially closed its doors in Saint John. The future would no longer involve transporting vast quantities of New Brunswick timber to overseas markets and importing foodstuff from the West Indies. Canadian grain and manufactured goods would soon arrive on the Maritime coast, transported by iron rails and supported by tariffs erected by the National Policy. Change would be sudden as the age of sail faded with every steam whistle heard in the distance. And while local markets were soon flooded with these new products, both Moncton and Saint John managed to embrace the challenge—Moncton by becoming headquarters and repair centre for the ICR, and Saint John by becoming CP's eastern terminus and Canada's Winter Port. Towns and villages in 19th century New Brunswick lobbied hard for a railway line because the life and death of each community was seen as at stake. Without a railway, people would simply leave, and so politicians were adamant that their region needed public funds to help build an iron connection to the outside world.

Prior to Confederation, New Brunswick had announced the Facility Act that offered a $10,000 per mile subsidy for railway construction as well as a $20,000 bonus for building into Quebec to connect with the Grand Trunk Railway. The province didn't have the cash to back up the new construction the Act initiated but did have lots of land. The province quickly switched the subsidy to 10,000 acres per mile. A number of railway companies, especially Alexander Gibson's New Brunswick Land and Railway Company (later called the New Brunswick Railway), took advantage of the subsidy, amassing huge land tracts north of Fredericton. During the Confederation debates, New Brunswick was already the owner and operator of the European and North American Railway between Shediac and Saint John and was anxious to have the line extended to Boston and Montreal. But New Brunswick was really more than eager to get out of the huge financial burden of building and operating railways. Politicians sensed an opportunity to negotiate a deal whereby the new Dominion would take over operations of New Brunswick's ENAR line. This became one of the terms of New Brunswick's entry into Confederation along with the construction of the Intercolonial Railway from Rivière-du-Loup through to Halifax. And in 1869, before the ICR was finished, the Dominion Government assumed operational responsibility for the ENAR. If the small branch lines within New Brunswick were built without sound economics, surely the ICR trunk line anchoring the entire rail system was built in a logical fashion, based on population statistics, and firm traffic demands. It doesn't seem so. The obvious direction for an intercolonial railway through New Brunswick in the late 1860s was up the St. John River Valley from Saint John to Edmundston and through the wilderness to Rivière-du-Loup. Yet the

Dominion of Canada was disinterested in the whole route affair—they wanted a confederation of British North American but cared little for details such as preferred railway routes—except as it pertained to construction costs. They simply didn't want to pay. Nova Scotia wanted a route that favoured Halifax as the most direct route to Montreal while New Brunswick insisted on the more heavily populated St. John River Valley route. But British North American in the 1860s was still a ward of an overseas power that was willing to pay significant construction costs if it got its way in selecting the route to the east coast.

In this railway debate, it wasn't so much that Nova Scotia won but that Britain got its' way. Britain saw a new powerful empire emerging out of the ashes of the American Civil War, one that was capable of mounting a major revenge attack on British North American for its role in assisting the rebel American south during the civil war. The St. John River Valley was deemed dangerously close to the Maine border. Consequently, British authorities selected the remote north shore route from the Maritimes to Rivière-du-Loup. The Halifax to Quebec route was a boom to Moncton and the north shore, yet did little to assist Saint John and the river valley in advancing their business opportunities north with the Canadas. While the Dominion with British capital was building the ICR to the Maritimes, the New Brunswick Legislature was announcing subsidy after subsidy to assist local entrepreneurs to build connecting lines to feed into the ICR. At Dalhousie, Chatham, Kent Junction, Sackville, Salisbury, Petitcodiac, Norton, and Hampton, branch lines were hastily constructed in the 1870s to link small villages with the ICR.

The ICR trunk line was a great financial boom to the province and connecting into the ICR would capitalize on the new transportation system that was changing travel from days and weeks into minutes and hours. A previous two-day stagecoach ride in the 1840s from Saint John to Moncton was now a two to four hour affair. And a Petitcodiac to Moncton train ride was minutes by steam power instead of four hours by horse power. The coming of the railway to New Brunswick meant the world was changing rapidly and the choice was to hop onto the new travel machine or stay in the past. Most New Brunswickers wanted in and railway promoters were building lines in all directions. The Dominion's public railway, the ICR, had been built through eastern New Brunswick largely at the expense of the St. John River Valley. But the next large railway into the province was a very different business.

In 1885, the privately funded Canadian Pacific managed to reach the Pacific from Montreal and Canada's first transcontinental railway began to build east to complete the great east-to-west railway. Like a decade earlier, politicians of every stripe lobbied furiously for the CP to build through their community. Even Prime Minister Sir John A. Macdonald fought hard for the line to be built through the center of the province from Grand Falls to Fredericton, and on to Salisbury and Moncton where it could connect into the ICR and on to the port of Halifax. In the end, Canadian Pacific, being a private enterprise, decided on the most cost-effective route to the east coast and built through Maine to McAdam and down to Saint John. CP's great economic advantage was its' "Short Line" to the coast, and this advantage over the Intercolonial Railway was of great benefit to Saint John.

If the coming of Canadian Pacific to New Brunswick proved to be of great value to the province, the next great transcontinental railway to arrive did so with mixed benefits. By 1900, too much of a good thing characterized the railway industry in eastern North American and the publicly funded National Trans-continental Railway became Canada's third transcontinental line. While it could be justified in the fast growing western regions of Canada, it was extended into eastern Canada as a political afterthought. It was simply not needed. The NTR struggled to find a reliable operator after the Grand Trunk realized it would lose too much money if it assumed operations, and reneged on accepting the leasing agreement.   During World War I, the federal government rolled the orphan NTR into the ICR operations throughout eastern Canada. And in 1918, a huge new government railway was launched. Canadian National Railway spent much of the 1920s and 1930s merging and consolidating rail lines until the arrival of World War II demanded a new expansion of the Canadian railway system to meet the needs of the Allied war effort.

And if the 1940s were the railway industry's true but temporary moments of glory—moving record amounts of freight and passengers—the 1950s became the beginning of the end for Canada's railway system as an essential piece of the national fabric. Cars, trucks, and airplanes were stealing the show. And if all things—good and bad—must pass, then on April 25, 1960, the steam age of Canada's railway officially came to an end when Canadian National Steam Engine No. 6043 ended her regular run as she pulled into Winnipeg amid much fanfare, and rolled under a banner that read: "Farewell to 6043 C.N.R.'s Last Steam Locomotive." Canada's other national railway, Canadian Pacific, also abandoned the steam engine the same year. And with the end of steam locomo-tion came the beginning of the end of the great age of the railway. Within a few short decades, the actual trackage of operational railways in New Brunswick would be down to a few hundred miles from a peak of over two thousand miles of operating tracks in the 1920s.

A Railway Compendium

ALBERT RAILWAY COMPANY — This branch railway was opened in 1876 between Salisbury and Albert Mines. It was renamed the Salisbury and Harvey Railway after new owners took the line over in 1884. The railway was extended to Alma with a branch to Harvey Bank in 1892 under another business name, Albert Southern Railway. But the southern section closed in 1900 due to a lack of business. The original line was also in trouble financially and in 1909, acquired new owners as well as a new name—the Salisbury and Harvey Railway. The railway was purchased by the federal government in 1918 for $75,000 and became part of Canadian National Railway before being abandoned in 1989. Recently, the Salem and Hillsborough Railroad operated a short excursion train for visitors to Albert County.

AROOSTOOK RIVER BRANCH RAILWAY — In 1876, as Alexander Gibson's New Brunswick Railway was being built north to Edmundston, the company built a five mile spur line up the river to Tinker where it met the Aroostook River Railway from Caribou.

BEERSVILLE COAL & RAILWAY — This short, 6.5-mile spur line was constructed in Kent County in 1904 to move coal to Adamsville where the railway would connect with the ICR running north from Moncton. The railway was built cheap, including second-hand rails acquired from the ICR, and eventually went bankrupt while the rails were taken up in 1929.

BOUCTOUCHE AND MONCTON BRANCH RAILWAY — This little 32-mile branch line operated under various ownerships between 1894 and 1965. It was also called the Moncton and Bouctouche Railway as well as the Moncton and Northumberland Strait Railway Company.

CALAIS STREET RAILWAY — In 1893, a joint Calais–St. Stephen electric streetcar railway was launched serving the two border communities as well as the two upper Milltowns. The Calais-St. Stephen Street Railway service remained the key affordable transportation option for residents of both sides of the border until a bus service was introduced in 1931.

CANADA EASTERN RAILWAY COMPANY — This line from outside Chatham to Gibson on the north side of Fredericton was built as a partnership between two railway tycoons, Alexander Gibson and Senator Jabez Snowball. The 150-mile railway, originally called the Northern and Western Railway, opened in 1887, and was extended east of Chatham to Loggieville in 1894. The two partners quarrelled and Gibson boycotted the railway, refusing to ship his Marysville mill cotton products through his own rail line until Snowball agreed to sell his shares. Gibson had won the match and renamed the line the Alexander Gibson Railway and Manufacturing Company. But in 1904, the railroad was again called the Canada Eastern Railway, and was in deep financial trouble until the federal government bought Gibson out. The line then became part of the ICR/CNR network and remained in operation until 1985 when the section east of McGivney was abandoned.

CANADIAN ATLANTIC RAILWAY — CPR established this east coast division in 1988 as they faced the prospects of declining traffic and major demands for infrastructure improvements. With aging bridges and trackage needing to be rebuilt, CP began the process of selling their east coast rail system to short line operators.

CANADIAN NATIONAL RAILWAY — Canada's public railway was born in 1918 and became the operator of a vast network of private railways that had been acquired with federal funds by the Canadian Government Railways. CN would continue to acquire private lines with dubious prospects well into the 1930s. At its' peak in the early 1950s, CN employed over 100,000 workers, maintained 5,000 stations, 121,000 freight cars, and 3,600 passengers cars. Nearly 7,000 bridges were maintained while transporting 80 million tons of freight annually, and 18 million passengers. With 1,400 printed rail schedules, CN transported 24 million express parcels, transmitted 14 million messages, and managed to accommodated three quarters of a million guests in its' hotels. CN was huge— nothing of this magnitude had existed in Canada before and probably never again. It was the largest company in the country and one of the largest railways in the world. Its' influence was massive and when the elephant sneezed, Canadians feared the consequences. Layoffs in 1950s meant 30,000 less workers but CN still entered the 1960s suffering from too much capacity—trackage, rolling stock, and employees. The historic Canadian railway became a publicly traded company in the 1990s and a book detailing the adventure was published called *The Pig That Flew*.

CANADIAN PACIFIC RAILWAY — After CPR reached the Pacific coast in 1885, they acquired a number of long term leases in western and central New Brunswick. This allowed CPR to patch together a rail line in 1889 from Montreal through Maine to Saint John. CPR was Canada's first transcontinental railway and the beaver was adopted as the railway's logo since it was seen as a national symbol. By the 1920s, most railways in the province were either part of the CP system or operated by CN. At its' peak in the early 1940s, Canadian Pacific employed over 60,000 workers but in the 1990s, CP downsized its operations and abandoned or sold all its' lines east of Montreal.

CARAQUET AND GULF SHORE RAILWAY COMPANY — The first 20 miles of the Caraquet Railway on the north shore opened in 1895 between Gloucester Junction and Stonehaven. By 1898, the remaining section all the way to Shippagan was completed but struggled to break even and was amalgamated with the Gulf Shore Railway in 1911. By 1918, the Dominion government was buying branch lines throughout eastern Canada and the owners agreed to sell out for $200,000. CN ran the line until abandoning the railway in the early 1990s.

CARLETON BRANCH RAILWAY — The small 3.5-mile railway was built by a group of West Saint John businessmen with financial assistance from the City of Saint John. It connected the Western Extension Railway that had ended near the Reversing Falls with the west side docks. The line became part of the Saint John and Maine Railway in 1880 and was acquired by the federal government in 1885 after the new railway bridge was erected at the Reversing Falls. The line was then leased out to the New Brunswick Railway and folded into CP's operations in 1889. Eventually, the CPR built two deep water docks at Sand Point that helped make Saint John a major winter port.

CENTRAL RAILWAY COMPANY, THE NEW BRUNSWICK COAL AND RAILWAY COMPANY AND THE FREDERICTON AND GRAND LAKE COAL AND RAILWAY COMPANY — The idea behind the Central Railway was to link Fredericton with the head of Grand Lake and on through to connect with the ICR railway from Saint John to Moncton. The section from Chipman south to Norton was opened in 1888 and the 15-mile route from Chipman to Minto and the Newcastle coal fields in 1894. The latter was called the Grand Lake Coal Railway while the entire Chipman to Fredericton section had been incorporated as a separate company called the New Brunswick Coal and Railway Company. Later it was called the Fredericton and Grand Lake Coal and Railway Company, but was not fully completed through to Fredericton until 1913 when CP took over the operations of the entire Central Railway under long-term leases. Many of the wooden bridges were difficult for CP to maintain and could not support their heavy locomotives. In 1967, the Norton to Pennlyn section was abandoned and in the 1980s, almost the entire line was demolished or abandoned.

CHATHAM BRANCH RAILWAY—Senator Jabez Snowball built this railway from his hometown of Chatham in 1870 west to connect with the ICR at Derby Junction. In 1884, Snowball joined forces with Alexander Gibson to build a railway from Chatham all the way to Fredericton north. This railway, the Canada Eastern Railway, opened in 1887 and Snowball's Chatham Branch Railway was incorporated into the CER.

DALHOUSIE BRANCH RAILWAY — The Dalhousie Railway Company was formed in 1873 in order to build a branch railway west to connect Dalhousie with the Intercolonial Railway. Passenger service began in 1884 and the line was soon part of the ICR.

EUROPEAN AND NORTH AMERICAN RAILWAY — Construction began on the line in 1853 at both Saint John and Point-du-Chêne. It struggled with financial issues and was finally completed in 1860 by the Province of New Brunswick. In 1869, as part of New Brunswick's agreement to enter into Confederation, the ENAR became part of the federal ICR system.

FREDERICTON AND ST. MARY'S RAILWAY BRIDGE COMPANY — Incorporated in 1885 and backed financially by Sir John A. Macdonald's Dominion government, the Fredericton Railway Bridge was opened to traffic in 1887, and allowed the north side rail lines direct access to downtown Fredericton. But the federal government held the mortgage and foreclosed on the bridge owners in 1904. The next year, the government's ICR was in charge of operating the crossing. In 1936, the bridge was swept away in a big spring flood. A second railway bridge was built in 1938 and remains standing today.

FREDERICTON BRANCH RAILWAY — Built by the Fredericton Railway Company, the 22-mile Fredericton Branch Railway connected the capital city to Hartts Mills (Fredericton Junction) when it opened for traffic in 1869. The railway linked Fredericton with the Western Extension Railway from Saint John to Bangor and was eventually taken over by the CPR.

GRAND SOUTHERN RAILWAY — In 1882, this railway between St. Stephen and Saint John officially opened at a cost of $1,000,000 with government subsidies contributing almost $400,000. Yet the line lost money from the outset even though it was much quicker to the border than the old line going up to McAdam and back down to St. Stephen. The railway changed hands a number of times and became known as the Shore Line Railway in 1889. Later, the line was called the South Shore Railway. The railway was leased to CP but portions were abandoned first in the 1930s, then in the 1950s, and finally fully closed in the 1980s.

INTERCOLONIAL RAILWAY — The original ICR line from Halifax through to Rivière-du-Loup along the north shore opened to traffic in 1876. As the Dominion government's official railway in eastern Canada with headquarters at Moncton, the company acquired a number of other railways including the European and North American Railway. The ICR was the forerunner to today's Canadian National Railway.

INTERNATIONAL RAILWAY COMPANY OF NEW BRUNSWICK — Incorporated in 1885, the railway was not fully completed from Campbellton to Saint Léonard until 1910. Both the federal and provincial governments assisted in the construction that was designed to connect with the CPR and NTR at Saint Léonard, allowing for movement of freight from the north shore into the upper St. John River Valley. After a bridge was constructed across the St. John River, the International Railway could then connect with the Bangor and Aroostook Railway in Maine. In 1914, the line was purchased by Ottawa for $2,700,000, and became part of Canadian National after World War I. By 1989, the IRC had been abandoned.

KENT NORTHERN RAILWAY COMPANY — This railway connecting Richibucto with Kent Junction and the ICR opened in 1883 with assistance from the province of $5,000 per mile. Struggling to break even, the Northern Railway was sold and reorganized as the Kent Northern Railway in 1903 and again in 1911. World War I created increased traffic along the line but the 1920s were hard years. In 1929, the CNR purchased the railway for $60,000 and operated it until 1989.

MONCTON AND NORTHUMBERLAND STRAIT RAILWAY COMPANY — Originally called the Bouctouche and Moncton Branch Railway, the line opened in 1887 to serve the area along the Northumberland Strait above Shediac. New York interests acquired the 32-mile line in 1894, renamed it the Moncton and Bouctouche Railway, and attempted to extend the line north to Richibucto. This prompted another name change—Moncton and Northumberland Strait Railway Company—yet there was little success in extending the line north. In 1918, the railway was acquired by the federal government and folded into CN's operations. It was abandoned in 1965.

MONCTON STREET RAILWAY — Moncton's public transportation service began in 1890 with R. J. Duffy's horse carriage and then in 1894, a street railway operated along Main Street. In 1911, the Electric Street Railway Company began operations taking railway workers up High Street to John Street and the new ICR Shops. In 1931, the motorized Grey Bus Line was launched and the electric tram service was soon discontinued.

NATIONAL TRANSCONTINENTAL RAILWAY — The NTR from Moncton through to Winnipeg and on to the Pacific opened in 1912 as Canada's third national railway. Controversial from the start—the Grand Truck refused to accept the leasing agreement—the orphan NTR became part of Canadian National Railway after World War I.

NEW BRUNSWICK AND CANADA RAILWAY — After reaching Woodstock in the 1860s, the St. Andrews and Quebec Railway had been reorganized and renamed the New Brunswick and Canada Railway.

NEW BRUNSWICK AND PRINCE EDWARD ISLAND RAILWAY COMPANY — In 1883, the Cape Tormentine Branch Railway opened the first 18 miles to Baie Verte while the full 36 miles to Cape Tormentine was finished in 1886. In 1914, the Dominion government purchased the entire line then known as the New Brunswick and Prince Edward Island Railway for $270,000. Three years later, the modern year-round ferry service under CN's management linking the Cape Tormentine line with Prince Edward Island came into effect, and remained the essential rail link with the island. After 1989, the railway and all rail operations on Prince Edward Island were abandoned.

NEW BRUNSWICK LAND AND RAILWAY COMPANY — The New Brunswick Railway was incorporated in 1870 under the direction of Alexander Gibson. Gibson had a falling out with the other directors in 1882 after the railway decided to convert from narrow gauge to standard gauge. Standard gauge it would be, and so Gibson sold his interest and the railway became the New Brunswick Railway. This railway undertook a major expansion program by purchasing and leasing numerous lines in western New Brunswick before being absorbed by the CPR.

NEW BRUNSWICK RAILWAY — This railway was also known as the New Brunswick Land and Railway Company and was built from the north side of Fredericton north to Edmundston. It opened in 1878 and acquired a number of local railways in western New Brunswick in the 1880s. It was nicknamed the patchwork railway before being acquired by Canadian Pacific to serve as part of the Short Line between Montreal and Saint John.

NEW BRUNSWICK SOUTHERN RAILWAY — In 1994, CP rail retreated from the Maritimes and J.D. Irving acquired operating rights for most of the CP tracks in New Brunswick including the 84-mile trunk line from Saint John to St. Croix near McAdam. The Saint John based NBSR become owner and operators of the old Western Extension Railway that had served as CP's main line in and out of New Brunswick for over one hundred years. New Brunswick Southern Railway also acquired the old St. Stephen Branch Railway that extended 31 miles from St. Stephen to McAdam while a NBSR subsidiary, the Eastern Maine Railway, became the operator of the Maine portion of the old Western extension line from Vanceboro 105 miles to Brownville Junction.

PETITCODIAC AND ELGIN RAILWAY COMPANY — This 14-mile line was opened in 1876 amid turmoil over payment to the builder. Yet in 1878, a second spur line totalling 12 miles was erected north of Petitcodiac to Havelock. The full 26-mile railway was then called the Elgin, Petitcodiac and Havelock Railway Company but went into receivership in 1890. For a time, the line was owned and operated by Leonard Tilley. The railway was finally sold to the federal government at the end of World War II for $30,000. The Elgin section was abandoned in the 1950s while the Havelock line was closed around 2000.

SAINT JOHN AND QUEBEC RAILWAY: THE VALLEY LINE — The first 120 miles of tracks between Westfield along the St. John River Valley to Centreville was completed in 1914 but construction beyond Centreville was suspended after the champion of the valley railway, Premier J. Kidd Flemming, was found guilty of political extortion and resigned from office. The CPR bought the line in 1929 for $6,000,000 and operated the passenger service until the 1950s. Parts of the line still transported freight for CP until the 1980s.

SAINT JOHN STREET RAILWAY — The Peoples Street Railway Company was first formed in 1866 and consisted of a horse-drawn streetcar. In 1886, the Saint John Street Railway became operational as an electric streetcar service. The service lasted into the 1930s but in 1914, the province's worst labour conflict took place in the streets of Saint John after a dispute between the company and its' workers erupted into a bloody riot.

SOUTHAMPTON RAILWAY COMPANY — This 13-mile line from Millville to Southampton on the St. John River was completed in 1913. It was built by local entrepreneurs but operated by CP under a long-term lease. The line was essentially operated for the St. Anne Nackawic paper mill for much of the 1900s until abandoned in the late 1990s.

ST. ANDREWS AND QUEBEC RAILWAY — New Brunswick's first railway was incorporated in 1835 with work beginning in 1847, and completed 15 years later from St. Andrews to Richmond Corner near Woodstock. This line had started out at Passamaquoddy Bay before going bankrupt after reaching Woodstock in the 1860s. Renamed the New Brunswick and Canada Railway, the line joined the New Brunswick Railway at Woodstock going north to Grand Falls and Edmundston. In 1882, it was leased to the New Brunswick Railway and became part of CP's operations in 1889.

ST. JOHN BRIDGE AND RAILWAY EXTENSION COMPANY — A cantilever-type railway bridge over the Reversing Falls was built in 1885 and the same year, a rail line from the terminus of the Western Extension on the west side across the river to Saint John was finally connected to the ICR. This meant that Halifax, Moncton, Saint John, Maine, and Montreal were finally connected by a single rail. CPR acquires the St. John Bridge and Railway Extension Company through a stock purchase in 1905, and ended up controlling the trackage from the Reversing Falls to Long Wharf. A second bridge replacing the 1885 structure was completed in 1921 and remains open today.

ST. MARTINS RAILWAY COMPANY — The St. Martins and Upham Railway was incorporated in 1871 and opened in 1878 from St. Martins to Hampton where the ICR line ran from Saint John to Moncton. Most years saw expenses exceeding revenue and the Central Railway acquired the line in 1887 through a lease and operated it as their southern line. The Central Railway Company had little luck making the railway work and gave it back to the owners in 1897. The line was then sold and renamed the St. Martins Railway. In 1918, the little railway was again sold, this time to the Dominion government, and given to the CNR who operated the line until it was abandoned in 1940.

St. Stephens Branch Railway — In 1866, the St. Stephen Branch Railway Company opened a 19-mile branch line from Watt Junction on the St. Andrew and Quebec Railway line into St. Stephen. Later, the line went up to McAdam and connected over into Maine as well as back to Saint John. In 1889, the St. Stephens Branch Railway became part of the CP system after having been taken over by the New Brunswick Railway.

Temiscouata Railway — This line was incorporated with a plan to extend from Rivière-du-Loup to Edmundston since the New Brunswick Railway had declined to build beyond Edmundston. The 82-mile stretch was completed in 1889, and later the Quebec entrepreneurs extended the line 27 miles to Conners in Madawaska County. Yet the projected lumber traffic up to the St Lawrence failed to occur and the line struggled to pay its way. The railway was reorganized a number of times and portions were closed but after World War II, CN purchased the Temiscouata Railway for $480,000. Between the 1970s and the 1990s, the entire line was gradually abandoned.

Tobique Valley Railway Company — This 28-mile railway along the Tobique River was constructed in 1894 mainly to access gypsum at Plaster Rock. The line was built by New Brunswickers but leased to Canadian Pacific. While new owners came on board in 1936, CP continued to operate the line until it was abandoned in the late 1990s.

Western Extension Railway — The European and North American Railway from west Saint John to McAdam was opened in 1869 while the ENAR Western Extension into Maine through to Bangor was completed in 1871. The Western Extension was sold to railway promoter Murray Kay's Saint John and Maine Railway Company in 1878. Four years later, the Maine section was acquired by the Maine Central Railway. Eventually the Western Extension became part of CP's operations.

York and Carleton Railway Company — This little 10-mile railway from Cross Creek Station in York County was opened to traffic in 1901 as far as Stanley and then on to Ryans Creek in 1909. In 1918, the federal government gave the owners $18,000 for the line that became part of CN's operation until it was abandoned in 1986.

EARLY YEARS IN CHARLOTTE COUNTY

St. Andrews Railway Station, c1889

No. 12 locomotive is shown on the tracks in the foreground. New Brunswick's first railway came out of the resort town of St. Andrews and the originals of the St. Andrews and Quebec Railway go back to the 1820s—the dawn of the railway era. The decade marked the beginning of the steam locomotion age as George Stephenson's radical new steam engine Locomotion haul freight and passengers for the first time on the British Stockton and Darlington Railway. In 1827, a group of St. Andrews businessmen approached colonial authorities in Britain for assistance in building a railway that would link the east coast of British North America to Quebec. These citizens were keenly aware that the first to make the inland connection would have a freight and passenger monopoly for at least part of the year when the St. Lawrence River remained frozen. Since St. Andrews possessed an ice free port all-year round, shipping goods to Europe and America by rail from the Canadas in winter seemed a lucrative goal. Quebec City was a mere 200 miles along a straight line. But British authorities rejected the proposal because their military officials favoured a rail line far away from the American border.

It was not until 1835 that the St. Andrews and Quebec Railway Company was formed and a railway survey was conducted measuring 195 miles. The line began at Point Lévis opposite Quebec City, across the St Lawrence foothills, the northern Appalachians through Mars Hill, and down to St. Andrews. But investors were hesitant to get involved since the problem was that no one knew for certain where northern Maine began and ended. Officials in both Washington and London had simply no agreement on a fixed border for northwestern New Brunswick and Northern Maine. The land from the St. Lawrence to the headwaters of the St. Croix River had not been surveyed, and the Mars Hill area was especially problematic because both regions claimed the area. But in 1842, the Ashburton Treaty settled the borders of Quebec, Maine and New Brunswick with Mars Hill awarded to Maine. This resulted in more than half of the 1837 survey line being situated in Maine.

Railway Trestle, St. Andrews Waterfront, c1890

During the 1840s, railway construction was booming in the United States and British private capital became interested in investing in colonial railway projects as long as they were built within British North America. In 1847, with British private backing and support from the New Brunswick Legislature, the St. Andrews and Quebec Railway Company broke ground in St. Andrews with the intention of building a rail line to Woodstock. Irish immigrant workers provided the labour and slowly, very slowly, a railway began to be constructed north from St. Andrews. A locomotive costing $5,000 was ordered in 1850 and the company built with iron rails on the broad gauge (5'6") but ran out of money a number of times, finishing a mere twelve miles by 1852. Despite being broke and beaten in building a railway to the Atlantic—the Montreal to Portland line had been completed in 1853—the St. Andrews entrepreneurs continued on, vowing to be the first to build to the St. Lawrence through British North American territory.

With new financing and a new name, the New Brunswick and Canada Railway, the first 34 miles of track were opened in 1857 and the next year, the 65 miles from St. Andrews to Canterbury opened with much fanfare despite the fact the company was broke and few workers had been paid. Another four years of difficulties saw the line completed to Richmond Corner outside of Woodstock but the New Brunswick and Canada Railway then defaulted on its bond and was placed in receivership. New Brunswick's first railway had ground to a halt far from the St. Lawrence after decades of attempts and half-starts, building a line from the Atlantic to the St. Lawrence River. And it would another 25 years before a railway would reach though to Upper Canada.

Old Algonquin Hotel, St. Andrews, c1905

In 1871, the Maine Western Extension line from Bangor to Vanceboro opened connecting across the border to McAdam and Saint John. The New Brunswick and Canada Railway from St. Andrews also connected into this railway grid and for the first time, the little pristine community on Passamaquoddy Bay had direct connections with the large cities of eastern North America. While the Algonquin Hotel was not finished until 1889, St. Andrews' future as a sea-side resort community was made possible by the completion of the Western Extension Railway. Since the Fundy shore offered a pollution free environment—absolute hay fever exemption became one of the community's advertising slogans—visitors from New York, Boston, and Montreal began to travel by rail to St. Andrews for clean air holidays. A newspaper in Saint John even declared St. Andrews the "watering place of the Dominion."

In the early 1870s, a number of prominent citizens formed the St. Andrews Hotel Company, building the Argyll Hotel but a second enterprise, the St. Andrews Land Company including Sir Leonard Tilley and a number of prominent Americans, took over the hotel company and built a number of cottages and homes for summer visitors. In 1889, the Algonquin opened to great acclaim as the CPR had acquired all trackage of the New Brunswick Railway including the line into St. Andrews. The first CPR train arrived filled with summer guests on July 1st. In 1902, the Algonquin was purchased by CP and operated as one of their premier resort hotels along with Banff Springs, Lake Louise, and Chateau Frontenac in Quebec City. Despite a fire in 1914, the hotel was rebuilt the next year and remained a treasured CP resort until 1970. Today, the old Algonquin is the property of the Province of New Brunswick.

Sir William Van Horne, c1900

One of Canada's most celebrated 19th century builders, William Van Horne, was responsible for the construction of the Canadian Pacific Railway, Canada's first transcontinental railway. In the 1880s, Van Horne was one of many visitors to St. Andrews and he purchased six hundred acres on Minister's Island. He soon began building a large summer estate named Covenhoven. William Van Horne was president of CP in 1899 when it acquired most of the rail lines in western New Brunswick, and each summer throughout the 1890s, Van Horne and his family would travel in his private railcar named *Saskatchewan* to St. Andrews, spending their summers at Covenhoven. Van Horne retired from the CPR in 1899 and spent more time at Minister's Island constructing a 28-room mansion that was finally completed in 1901. He later became involved in railway construction in Cuba and his restless energy remained with him all his life. He was a larger-than-life character that loved grandeur and thought big—large trains, spacious stations, and huge buildings appealed to him. His greatest feat was no doubt building the CPR to the Pacific. He died in 1915.

Bar Road Halt, St. Andrews, c1900

This tiny railway stop outside St. Andrews was built especially for Sir William Van Horne, president of Canadian Pacific, after he purchased one end of nearby Minister's Island and constructed a summer estate. As the head of CPR, Van Horne lived in Montreal and when he and his family traveled to his elaborate estate called Covenhoven, horse and carriages would gather at the Bar Road Halt and convey the party across the exposed sand bar to the island. Always a railroad man, Van Horne would time his arrival at Bar Road to coincide with low tide on Passamaquoddy Bay so that he would not have to wait before being escorted across the exposed channel to Minister's Island. Van Horne's time at Covenhoven was spent on farming and being a horticulturist. He spared no expense and built extensive barns and outbuildings, importing a special breed of cattle from Europe and growing many unique fruits and vegetables. Guests were always welcome and encouraged to see Covenhoven for themselves. Most visitors came away impressed and amazed at what Van Horne had managed to accomplish during his two decades at Minister's Island.

Railroad on the Calais Waterfront, St. Stephen Wharves in the Background, c1890

In the 1850s, as the St. Andrews and Quebec Railway slowly proceeded north towards Woodstock, businessmen in St. Stephen and Calais realized that their railway hopes had been dashed. Their international community would not be the entry point for a railway from New Brunswick through to Bangor and Boston. Entrepreneurs in Calais had built the Calais & Penobscot Railroad from the Calais wharves along the St. Croix River but the railroad lacked a connection west through to Bangor and Boston. Consequently, an opportunity appeared from the Canadian side. In 1866, the St. Stephen Branch Railway Company constructed a rail line 19 miles north along the St. Croix River to Watt Junction, connecting with the St. Andrews and Quebec Railway line. And in 1871, the Western Extension of the European and North American Railway finally linked Saint John with Bangor crossing the border at McAdam Junction across to Vanceboro.

The St. Stephen Branch Railway along with the old St. Andrews and Quebec Railway all linked into the line forty miles above St. Stephen at McAdam, making St. Stephen the lone railway option for all border residents travelling to Boston. In 1882, the Grand Southern Railway to Saint John along the Fundy coast was also opened. And St. Stephen would retain its border railway superiority until 1897 when the Washington County Railroad constructed a line through to Ellsworth that finally connected Calais to Bangor.

Canadian Pacific Ticket Agent, Calais, c1895

Calais lacked rail links to Bangor, Boston or Montreal until 1897, and so the St. Stephen Branch Railway began offering US citizens passenger service to the outside world. Calais had wanted a rail connection across the bridge at Ferry Point to link into the St. Stephen Branch Railway but the existing wooden bridge lacked the proper structural support. A new steel bridge would not be built until 1895, in time for the opening the Calais-St. Stephen Street Railway. When Canadian Pacific acquired much of the railway trackage in western New Brunswick in 1889, including both the St. Stephen Branch Railway and the Grand Southern Railway, they opened this ticket agency on Lower North Street in Calais. And for a decade, in Calais-St. Stephen, Canadian Pacific enjoyed a railroad monopoly. CP's only transportation competition involved steamships but while freight and passenger rates were generally lower by water, railway service was faster and less weather dependent.

Calais-St. Stephen Street Railway, Water Street, St. Stephen, c1905

In 1894, a 7-mile electric street railway opened encompassing Calais, St. Stephen, and the two upriver mill towns. In order to accommodate all legal requirements involved in 19th century international business affairs, two incorporations—one Canadian and one US—were organized with the St. Stephen company then leased over to the Calais Street Railway Company who ended up operating the railway. The street railway had required the construction of a new steel bridge at Ferry Point (both communities split the cost) replacing the old wooden structure. A full ride cost five cents, consisting of four miles in Maine and three miles in New Brunswick. The single car train ran from the Lower Wharf in Calais up to Milltown, Maine, across the Milltown Bridge into New Brunswick, and along the St. Croix River bank into downtown St. Stephen (as seen in this photograph) where it extended south, and connected with the Shore Line Railway on Prince William Street.

Once the new steel bridge was opened in 1895, connections from directly across to downtown Calais made the streetcar service quite efficient. The international electric street railway caused a sensation in the border area as picnics and all-day outings were extremely popular. Officials were not strict on applying riding restrictions and double and triple ride loops became common. Saturday nights' "go for a ride" outings were popular family entertainment in the Calais-St. Stephen community until the streetcar service was abandoned in 1929 due to the incoming Depression, and the popularity of the automobile.

Fifty-Fifth Battalion Boarding Train for Sussex, St. Stephen, May, 1915

Soldiers gather at the CPR Station on Water Street in St. Stephen before leaving for overseas duty. First stop was Sussex where a military assembly camp and training center served New Brunswick and eastern Canada throughout World War I. Over four thousands border residents including many Americans from Calais assembled that May day in 1915 to wish the soldiers a safe and speedy return back to the Maine-New Brunswick border community. Shortt's Military Band led the gathering into St. Stephen after church services in Milltown and many of the well-wishers handed out food baskets and cigars to local members of the 55th Battalion.

Shore Line Railway Station, c1890

This photo shows the tiny Shore Line station (later named the Grand Southern Railway) with the Union Jack flying overhead. After the European and North American Railway opened for traffic in 1860 between Saint John and Point-du-Chêne, more branch lines and extensions were planned including a railway west from Saint John to Maine. St. Andrews and St. Stephen-Calais were both thriving towns, and a 74-mile coastal rail line survey from Saint John to Calais had been undertaken in the early 1850s. But instead of heading west through Charlotte County, the Western Extension Railway was built north from Saint John towards Fredericton before heading west to meet the Maine Border at McAdam and Vanceboro. Yet Saint John railway promoter W.K. Reynolds still became determined to build a shore rail route to compete for freight and passengers with the coastal shippers. He had constructed the Saint John Suspension Bridge as well as the city's People's Street Railway and in 1872, the Grand Southern Railway was incorporated with a plan to construct an inexpensive, narrow-gauge, 80-mile rail line from West Saint John to St. Stephen.

Construction began in late 1877 but cash flow problems arose as well as a number of controversies around construction issues. In 1880, after the company converted the tracks to standard gauge, the line began to operate but it was not until 1882 that the Grand Southern Railway officially opened. The line had cost more than $1,000,000 to build ($400,000 was government funds) and immediately began to lose several thousand dollars each year. Reynolds and his partners finally gave up and sold the line. In 1889, it became known as the Shore Line Railway Company. And in 1900, the railway was renamed the South Shore Railway Company. The following year, the railway was taken over by the New Brunswick Southern Railway Company and then in 1911, Canadian Pacific became the operator. During the 1930s, some of the sections near St. Stephen were abandoned by CP and despite a large mill that operated at Lake Utopia, and the building of the nuclear plant at Point Lepreau, the Shore Line Railway ceased to exist by the 1980s.

EUROPEAN AND NORTH
AMERICAN RAILWAY

Old Hercules Engine at Point-du-Chêne, 1857

Hercules, one of New Brunswick's first wood-burning locomotives, is seen here being hauled by sled from Point-du-Chêne to Shediac to work the European and North American Railway during the winter of 1857. The ENAR was completed between Moncton and Point-du-Chêne in 1857, and connected to Saint John three years later. *Hercules* was one of two locomotives bought by the ENAR from Boston. *Hercules* was shipped to Point-du-Chêne on the Montezuma in 1854 before the railway had been constructed, and the second locomotive, *Samson*, was shipped up the Petitcodiac River and off-loaded at Moncton. Both engines remained in storage until the line opened in 1857. The ENAR rails were laid in the British broad gauge fashion (5' 6") but were later converted to standard gauge (4' 8.5") to allow for linking with other railway lines, especially in the United States since the majority of American railroads had been constructed on the standard gauge format. Most of the iron rails and fastenings were manufactured in Britain but the Phoenix Foundry in Saint John constructed a number of the other ENAR locomotives while the Harris & Allan and Frederick James companies of Saint John built the freight cars as well as the flat and passenger cars. The European and North American Railway was conceived by Saint John entrepreneurs and financed largely by the New Brunswick Legislature as a way to link the Gulf of St. Lawrence fishing communities with Saint John. The entrepreneurs also had plans to build to the Maine border where American railway builders had promised to build through to Bangor. But the railway west of Saint John, known as the Western Extension, would have to wait another decade before it would be completed.

Pointe-du-Chêne Wharf, Shediac, c1905

Pointe-du-Chêne's natural extension out into Shediac Bay was considered an ideal landing point for vessels sailing along the Northumberland Strait. In 1853, Pointe-du-Chêne was chosen as the location for establishing a terminal for the European and North American Railway. With railway connections out to the pier, the Pointe-du-Chêne wharf immediately became Shediac Bay's major port and substantial quantities of lumber, potatoes, and livestock were shipped from this site. In June of 1854, the Pointe-du-Chêne pier received the first wood-burning locomotive for the new railway and by Confederation, the wharf was booming with railway traffic and ferry service to Prince Edward Island, the Miramichi, and south to Pictou. It was not until 1917 that Prince Edward Island's year-round ferry link to the mainland was moved from here to the shorter connection at Cape Tormentine. This change hurt traffic at Pointe-du-Chêne but the pier had now become the gateway to New Brunswick's premier beach resort.

Pointe-du-Chêne, Shediac, 1931

The pier at Pointe-du-Chêne can be seen jutting far out into the channel of Shediac Bay with Shediac Island visible in the upper left corner. By 1900, the wharf and surrounding beaches had become a favourite picnic and vacation site for Monctonians. During the summer months, the Sunday picnic train to Pointe-du-Chêne had a carnival-like atmosphere, with up to twenty rail cars carrying beach-goers to nearby Belliveau Beach. The Sunday train would depart Moncton at 1:30 pm, after church services, and leave the pier for the half hour trip back to the city at 7:00 pm. But Pointe-du-Chêne's most notable era was around the time that this photo was taken in the early 1930s. Trans-Atlantic air service had developed using aircraft that landed on water and these flying boats needed a fog-free harbour. Pan American Airways choose Pointe-du-Chêne as its' Atlantic terminus and other airlines also began using Shediac Bay as a launching pad for flights to Europe.

ICR Station, Shediac, c1908

On August 1, 1860, the European and North America 120-mile Saint John to Shediac railway was officially opened to traffic and within two years, a roundhouse and additional repair shops were built at Shediac. Despite massive upheavals during the 1860s, including a recession, the American Civil War, and Confederation, Shediac remained a thriving railway town, and the headquarters of the line. Fish, lumber, agricultural produce, and some manufactured goods were shipped in significant quantities both in and out of the Pointe-du-Chêne terminal. And by the end of the decade, the ENAR line had been merged with the Intercolonial Railway that was proceeding slowing between Halifax and Quebec. Shediac still seemed vital to all future east coast railway plans despite suffering a huge loss to its wharf during the Great Saxby Gale of 1869. But 1872 brought a massive fire that destroyed the Shediac railway shops at the same time that an extensive push was being conducted throughout New Brunswick to complete the ICR under Sandford Fleming's leadership.

The great new line would link Upper Canada with Halifax, Saint John, and the United States. Unfortunately for Shediac, its shops were gone and the Intercolonial Railway commissioners chose Moncton over Shediac for the entire offices, repair shops, and machine works. And throughout the remaining years of the 1800s and well into the 20th century, growth stalled in Shediac and other Westmorland centres, as Moncton flourish to become the major railway centre of Canada's east coast. And despite Shediac remaining a shipping port, its future would be away from heavy industry. Instead of becoming the centre of the 19th century's greatest industry, Shediac would eventually become a big player in the 20th century's largest industry—tourism.

Railway Bridge Over the Scoudouc River, Shediac, c1906

Shediac's seaside location and proximity to Prince Edward Island, Cape Breton, Halifax, and New Brunswick's north shore meant that regular coastal trading within the Maritimes occurred well before 1800. A packet ship, *Delphin*, under Captain Anthony Simpson, began sailing between Shediac and Summerside prior to 1840, and soon after, small steamers began to provide regular ferry service between the two communities.

During the early railway era, the bustling seaport saw its future as offering Saint John merchants and inland farmers a convenient seaport terminus for exporting their products quickly out into the Gulf of St. Lawrence. In 1852, the first contract was signed for the construction of the European and North America Railway between Saint John and the Northumberland Strait. The town's old Queen's Wharf was judged unsuited for heavy railway traffic so British construction contractors selected a new site at Cape Brulé. But after work began, it was decided to abandon the location due to exposure to gale winds and the need to build too far out to reach deep waters. Thus Pointe-du-Chêne became the chosen site of Shediac Bay's new railroad wharf.

The celebrated politician, Albert James Smith, turned the first sod in 1853. On August 20, 1857, the first twenty miles of the line opened between Shediac and Moncton. At the time, Moncton's entire railway operation employed only two employees while Shediac's prosperity seemed assured with thirty-four employees working at repair shops, and four additional men employed at the Pointe-du-Chêne terminal. The inaugural train ride aboard *Hercules* was a grand day for citizens throughout Westmorland County and signal Shediac's entry into the modern world of steel and iron. Despite stopping along the way to refuel its log-burning engine, *Hercules* chugged along on that first day, speeding past Scoudouc, Painsec, Cook's Brook, Humphrey, and across the marsh at Sunny Brae, ending its first trip at the Main Street station in the little town of Moncton.

Petitcodiac Railway Station, c1912

The original train station at Petitcodiac was built in the late 1850s to accommodate the European and North America Railway between Saint John and Pointe-du-Chêne. It burned in the 1860s and this station was the second on the site. The maiden voyage of the first ENAR train made its way through Petitcodiac on July 18, 1860. While there was significant confusion about where exactly the rail line would come through the village, railway commissioner E.B. Chandler knew precisely the location since he had purchased land two miles upstream from the original village at the Pitfield land grant property. Once this property was picked as the site for the railway, Chandler profited immensely by selling building lots. By the time the Intercolonial Railway fully absorbed the ENAR in the mid-1870s, Petitcodiac was booming from the railway business.

Besides being the watering and fueling station for the railway, the village was shipping vast quantities of sawn lumber and a number of new businesses had relocated to the community. A branch rail line was built in 1876 southward from Petitcodiac to Elgin. The 14-mile spur line was built by local investors and helped along with a $70,000 provincial subsidy as well as assistance from the Elgin community. The line was affectionately known by locals as "The Prong" but the railway builders were never paid in full for building the Petitcodiac and Elgin Railway. Yet in 1878, a second spur line totalling 12 miles was erected north of Petitcodiac to Havelock. The full 26-mile railway was then called the

Elgin, Petitcodiac and Havelock Railway Company and only operated part of the year to keep costs down. Unfortunately, the line was never a money-maker and was placed in receivership in 1890. Sold a number of times, the branch railway was purchased by the Dominion government in 1918 for $30,000.

Saint John Milk Train, No. 22 Express, Sussex Station, c1912

One change that came with the arrival of railways in the 19th century was that milk was no longer transported long distances by horse and wagon. Spoilage became less common since milk transported by rail could be heated in the winter and packed in ice cars in the summer months. On the old Europe and North American Railway out of Saint John, the first morning train was always the milk train stopping at each small depot through the Kennebecasis Valley. The train collected fresh milk from the farmers and delivered the cans to the dairies in Sussex and Saint John. Collection was daily except on Sundays.

In her book, *Historic Sussex*, author Elaine Ingalls Hogg points out that Sussex was home to the province's first creamy in 1884 after a centrifugal cream separator was acquired from England. Later, Sussex established the first cheese factory in New Brunswick and a provincial dairy school. While other railways across the province also had milk runs, Sussex was the dairy capital of the province, and the early morning train through town also carried milk and other agricultural goods the other way into Moncton. The morning Moncton train west to Saint John also picked up milk for delivery in Saint John. Elaine Ingalls Hogg also mentions that Sussex resident John Sproule served as the milk train conductor in the late 19th century, and that milk trains through the Kennebecasis Valley lasted for almost 100 years. The first train through the valley occurred in 1860 and the last train to pick up and deliver milk was on May 31, 1957.

Cream Separator, Provincial Dairy School, c1899

Railway Station, Apohaqui, c1904

Standing in front of the station is Fred Morrison, railway station agent at Apohaqui. The station was built in 1859 and is now part of the agricultural museum in Sussex. Apohaqui in the Kennebecasis River Valley was once considered as Sir

Sandford Fleming's choice for the terminus of the Intercolonial Railway from Rivière-du-Loup. Three routes had been surveyed from Quebec including a border line close to the Maine-New Brunswick border, the so-called Robinson Route along the north shore (originally surveyed by Colonel Robinson), and the central line that Fleming had personally selected to run diagonally across New Brunswick to Apohaqui Station. The latter would then connect to the Saint John to Shediac ENAR line that had become part of the ICR in 1869. While the border route had been turned down as being too close to the hostile United States, Fleming's central line was not rejected for engineering reasons but by British officials intent on having the line run as far away from the United States as possible. Britain feared an invasion of Canada by the US and wanted to avoid having the trunk railway line within easy reach of the Maine border. Consequently, Apohaqui Station remained a small, insignificant railway stop on the old European and North American Railway line instead of becoming a major interconnecting hub of the Intercolonial Railway.

Intercolonial Railway Station, Hampton, c1905

This Isaac Erb photograph shows the station, freight shed, and water tower on the right along with the railway tracks leading out of town. An elevated platform for boarding and exiting the train is visible between the tracks and the station. Hampton is situated in the Kennebecasis Valley along the European and North America Railway route that was constructed through to Shediac in 1860. The village also served as the terminus of the St. Martins Railway that ran south to the Bay of Fundy. In 1869, the ENAR became part of the ICR and while the old ENAR had been constructed in the British broad gauge, once the ICR took over the line, it was converted to standard gauge. The old broad gauge had proved impractical when inter-lining with standard-gauge railways outside of New Brunswick. Once the conversion took place, freight out of eastern New Brunswick was able to move directly into the United States without having to be manually reloaded into standard-gauge freight cars.

European and North American Railway Station, Saint John, c1860

This dramatic Gothic revival structure was designed by Matthew Stead and completed in 1858 at the foot of Dorchester Street, near the terminus of the ENAR at Saint John's Long Wharf. Stead designed a number of Anglican churches in New Brunswick and his interest in neo-Gothic architecture was expressed in most of his work. This three-storey structure contained a ticket office, a general waiting room, a ladies waiting room, and toilets on the main floor as well as access to a long, covered track platform. The second floor included a private ladies room and railway offices, while the top floor served as the station master's apartment. The station remained Saint John's central railway centre until 1884 when a new railway station was built.

In 1853, construction on the ENAR began in Saint John and at Point-du-Chêne near Shediac under the direction of London capitalists with the goal of completing thirty miles per year. But work at both ends was stalled as inflation and labour expenses made the provincial subsidy of 6,500 pounds per mile uneconomical to continue. After work completely ground to a halt in 1855, New Brunswick bought out the London contractors and assumed full financial responsibility for construction of the line. In 1957, the Shediac to Moncton section opened as well as a small section east from Saint John. The next year, the Saint John to Rothesay portion was completed. And in 1860, the entire 108-mile route was finished and chief engineer Alexander Light had this to say in his final report. "The works of the railway now being virtually complete, it may not be out of place to remind you that... the trains have been run with marked regularity, and no accident endangering life or limb to passengers has occurred."

Prince of Wales Train, Opening of the ENAR, Rothesay, 1860

A number of men are dressed in formal top-hats standing on the tracks on the right. A gigantic decorated arch is visible in the background on the left. The European and North American Railway opened in 1860 and the Prince of Wales was visiting New Brunswick that summer. He was transported by a special train from Saint John to Rothesay (then called Kennebecasis Station) to help celebrate the occasion of the grand opening of New Brunswick's second railway. A written description from the period reveals the historic occasion and the reason for selecting the place name Rothesay: "The Prince of Wales having made known his intention of visiting the province in 1860, it was arranged that when going to Fredericton from Saint John his route should be via Kennebecasis Station and embark on board the "Forest Queen" at a wharf built by Hon J. Robertson. When setting about the plans and having failed on former occasions to agree on a name for the station and village, the expected arrival of the Prince was thought a good opportunity for doing so and Robert Thompson Sr. accordingly proposed Rothesay as being one of the Prince's oldest titles, as a fit name for the place of his embarkation and without one dissenting voice it was agreed upon. The Prince expressed himself pleased with the honour conferred on him"

Phoenix Foundry and Fleming's Locomotive Works, Saint John, 1901

The Fleming's Works site is behind the freight shed on the right. At least ten locomotive construction companies had set up operations throughout Canada before Confederation including the Phoenix Foundry in Saint John. George Fleming first served as a machinist's apprentice at the Dumferline Foundry in Scotland before working as a journeyman in Glasgow, Cork, Boston, and Baltimore. He established the Phoenix Foundry in Saint John in 1835, one of ten iron and brass foundries in the port city during the 1850s, all featuring some Scottish involvement in the various ownership structures. The foundries employed hundreds of workers and became the largest group of employers in Saint John by Confederation. Steam engines were largely replacing water-driven power at this time and the Phoenix Foundry became the largest local foundry as well as the first in New Brunswick to build steam locomotives.

In 1858, the foundry built the famous *Loostack* and *Ossekeag* steam engines that served on the Europe and North American Railway, featuring the common 4-4-0 wheel configuration. While the very early locomotives in the Maritimes were imported from Britain and then later from the United States, locomotives were also built at the Moncton ICR Shops and the Montgomery Iron Works in Halifax. Yet George Fleming's Phoenix Foundry was by far the largest producer of steam locomotives east of Montreal.

First European & North America Railway Roundhouse, Saint John, c1890

This George Taylor photograph shows the familiar domed engine house that was built by H.B. Crosby in 1859 near Brook Street and Gilbert's Lane on the ICR line east of the railway station at Saint John. The roundhouse was built in time for the opening of the European and North America Railway in 1860. The line from Shediac ended in east Saint John, and a roundhouse was necessary so that engines could turn around and be serviced at the same time. Roundhouses were not always necessary for turning engines around—a wye could also do the job whereby a Y-shaped track could be built at a right angle to the line, and the train could be diverted into the wye and driven past the fork. Once pass the fork of the wye, the tracks would be switched, and the train then backed on to the main line from the other side of the wye. And once the train had backed fully on to the main line, it would be facing the new direction, and be in position to return back along the rail line.

A wye was often built when there was limited amount of space for turning such as in Key West where the Florida East Coast Railway built a 128-mile rail line from south of Miami to Key West. The Florida railway had limited land and built wyes on trestles out over the sea for turning at Marathon and Key West. Yet at Saint John land space was not such an issue, and the ENAR roundhouse also served as the repair centre for the six locomotives employed on the line in the 1860s.

INTERCOLONIAL
RAILWAY

Intercolonial Railway Yard & Station, Moncton, c1877

This photograph by McKay Weldon was taken only one year after the opening of the Intercolonial Railway connecting the Maritimes with Upper Canada. The camera is looking west from Foundry Street onto the sprawling railway repair yards and train station. A Barnum's Circus billboard is visible on the building at the bottom right side of the photo. In the background on the right can be seen the ICR General Office and in the centre, the freight shed and railway station are visible. At a distance in the upper left corner, can be seen (note the chimneys) the oldest existing railway building in Moncton. Besides serving as a repair shop, the old brick building was used as a blacksmith shop, a paint shop and a horse barn. The famous structure was one of only a very few railway buildings that escaped the great 1906 railway fire. Moncton's growth in the 1870s and 1880s was fuelled by its selection as the headquarters and repair centre for the Intercolonial Railway, constructed between Halifax and Rivière-du-Loup. The official selection statement read: "The Governor in Council, having approved the recommendation of the Commissioners, having selected Moncton as the most suitable place for the erection of the principal work shops for the Government System of Railways." And when this federal announcement was made in 1871, this site was virtually empty and yet six years later, as this photo shows, the town had become a bee-hive of railway and industrial activity. And New Brunswick's pre-eminent railroad town would be incorporated into New Brunswick's third city in 1890.

Intercolonial Railway Group of Commissioners, c1879

The picture reveals the great Sir Sandford Fleming, chief commissioner of the Intercolonial Railway, seated with paper in hand. Other commissioners appointed by the federal privy council to build and manage the railway included Ontario politician, Aquila Walsh, Nova Scotian Archibald McLelan, Grand Trunk Manager, Charles Brydges, and New Brunswick's representative, Edward B. Chandler. In this picture, Chandler is standing behind Fleming. One of New Brunswick's fathers of Confederation and a prominent 19th century politician, E.B. Chandler played a decisive role in the establishment of the actual route of the ICR as it was cut south through New Brunswick. Selecting the route along New Brunswick's north shore as opposed to going along the St. John River

Valley was done by Fleming and Prime Minister Macdonald, with quite strong encouragement by the British Government since they were largely paying for the construction. But the question of whether the ICR would swing towards the coast below the Miramichi River and meet up in Shediac at the eastern extension of the European and North American Railway from Saint John, or go directly south from the Miramichi to Moncton, was a decision that the commissioners pondered for quite some time. Each commissioner seemed to have their own agenda, and Sir Sandford Fleming would do battle with the commission on everything from route changes, budget costs, and iron verses wood materials for the bridges. Yet Miramichi to Moncton was straighter than Miramichi to Shediac, and so the commissioners and Fleming agreed to this route but below Moncton, a battle erupted.

E.B. Chandler demanded that the railway pass through his hometown of Dorchester. Moncton to Sackville had been surveyed to run straight out to Painsec Junction and then down to Sackville, but Chandler was adamant that the line should curl west into Dorchester. Fleming refused to budge but after months of arguments and impasse, the commissioners finally backed Chandler. This meant that the ICR would be built an additional 14 kilometres via the Memramcook Valley to Dorchester. The gradients through this diversion were quite steep and building the trunk along this detour resulted in additional costs and construction delays. And even today, over 125 years after the zigzag line was completed, the extra time to travel by train from Sackville to Moncton is still significant.

Built about 1875, this building burned in 1882 and was replaced only to burn again in 1906. The ICR headquarters and office was located on Main Street near the railway station and the Brunswick Hotel. As Moncton's most prominent railway inn, the Brunswick Hotel competed for the train traveller business with its nearby rivals, the Windsor Hotel, American Hotel, and the Minto Hotel. The Brunswick Hotel began operations near the ICR station in the late 1870s to serve the railway. Called the Weldon House under its first owner Pat King, the building was purchased and renamed by George McSweeney in 1884. Under McSweeney's guidance, the Brunswick Hotel was refurnished and became ICR's preferred hotel for their travellers in the decades before the railway entered the hotel industry. The hotel boasted many modern conveniences for its

General Offices, Intercolonial Railway, Moncton, c1882

Brunswick Hotel, Moncton, c1905

time including a hot air furnace, special bathrooms, the city's first electric lights, as well as fine cuisine and was the site of many late Victorian balls and social engagements. A celebrated host and man-about-town, George McSweeney reportedly died tragically by chocking to death in front of hotel guests from swallowing a chicken bone. A major fire in 1891 to the wooden structure caused serious damages but the Brunswick Hotel was quickly repaired and then in 1919, was completely rebuilt of concrete and brick.

ICR Station, Moncton, c1900

This exceptional photograph was taken by noted Saint John photographer Isaac Erb. He left the notation: "a lot of trains in" to describe the photograph. Saint John architect John Dunn was influenced by the popular American architect H. Richardson and designed the building that the Rhodes, Curry Company of Amherst built in 1897. The photo shows a well-mannered late Victorian order to the new grounds and building. The station had been constructed opposite the Brunswick Hotel in the Romanesque Revival style arch revealed in the dormer windows. The station was considered so well designed in style and utility that stations built later at Pictou and Sydney simply used designs modified from the Moncton plans. This was Moncton's third railway station. The town's first passenger depot was completed in 1857 for the European and North American Railway and an earlier ICR station had opened in 1876. As headquarters and repair centre of the Intercolonial Railway, Moncton was the most important stop in the ICR system, and this station, located next to railway headquarters, was one of the largest built in the Maritimes. The grand old structure was eventually demolished and a new station was opened in 1963.

Old Union Station, Saint John, c1900

This Isaac Erb photograph shows Saint John's second railway station in splendid detail. Horse and carriages wait to take passengers into downtown Saint John. One of the terms of Confederation was that the Dominion government would take over existing railways in the east and that included the European and North American Railway. And in 1869, the ENAR was taken over by the federal government's Intercolonial Railway. Despite the fact that the ICR would not be completed for another seven years, the ICR now owned and operated the ENAR between Saint John and Shediac. Built in 1884 by the ICR, this stunning Romanesque Revival structure was constructed of stone by the Rhodes Curry Co. of Amherst and designed by J.T.C McKean.

The grand structure became a union station—shared by Canadian Pacific— after CP extended its service from the west side into downtown Saint John. The Mill Street three-story building included all the latest amenities of the 1880s, and fronted a 500-foot train shed where passengers could disembark or depart without getting wet if it rained. Baggage sheds where situated at each end of the train shed and this famous old station was one of Saint John's most enduring landmarks until it was replaced in 1923 by a new Union Station that was built and shared by Canadian National and Canadian Pacific.

Intercolonial Locomotive, Saint John, c1892

This photo from the James O'Donnell Collection in the New Brunswick Public Archives shows an old cold-burning locomotive, ICR No.100, with its' American wheel arrangement (4-4-0) in the Saint John ICR yard. In front of the engine would be the engineer, fireman, and perhaps the conductor or engineman, along with the young train-boy. On the right, looking serious are local train officials, no doubt the stationmaster, ticket agent, and perhaps the superintendent of the Saint John ICR operations. Steam engines were complicated machines in the 19th century, and a fast moving machine like a steam locomotive was considered dangerous to operate due to numerous head-on crashes.

Telegraph line along the rails had done much to cut down on accidents but an extensive whistle system had also been developed as a much needed safety measure. Locomotive whistle signals became important railway traditions with one short meaning stop and apply brakes immediately. Two long meant release brakes and go, while three short bursts signaled to back up if idle, and when running, to stop at the next station. Approaching a station was complicated: two long, one short, and one long, unless of course it was a very minor station or "whistle stop" that required a flag or lamp to be displayed before the train was required to stop. And gradually, as steam power had replaced water, wind, and horsepower, diesel engines replaced steam in the never-ending pursuit for productivity and efficiency. And yet for over one hundred years, steam power had effectively driven locomotives and revolutionized transportation as well as most aspects of 19th century life.

ICR Roundhouse, Saint John, c1900

Saint John's first roundhouse was built near Marsh Creek in 1859 as the western terminus of the European and North American Railway. This roundhouse replaced the old ENAR roundhouse that was so distinctive with a doom roof and turret. By 1900, when this photograph was taken, the ICR operations had engulfed a significant amount of operational landscape in Saint John extending over a mile east of Long Wharf past Marsh Creek. In additional to this roundhouse, the ICR grounds included the Union Station and freight elevator near Long Wharf as well as numerous additional freight sheds and repair shops. As well, the ICR had extended trackage from Marsh Creek along Courtenay Bay to reach the shipping piers at Lower Cove. Later, a rail trestle was extended across Lower Cover where a grain elevator was erected at the bottom of Water Street. While Moncton would remain the ICR headquarters and main repair centre, the coming of railway rival Canadian Pacific to West Saint John in 1889 spurred the ICR to expand their Saint John facilities while competing aggressively with CP for east coast freight and passenger service.

Freight Elevator, Intercolonial Railway, Saint John, c1920

This photo shows the ICR's old freight and grain elevator near Mill and Pond Streets that was connected to Long Wharf and could service ships docked in Saint John's Upper Cove area. This elevator burned and was replaced by a concrete structure at Reed's Point. On the far right can be seen the outer arch of Saint John's ICR Station, built in 1884 but by this time, was called Union Depot Station after the CPR and the ICR had agreed to share the facilities. After CPR's Short Line arrived in Saint John in 1889, transporting western grain was key to President Van Horne's east coast railway strategy. CPR managed to convince local authorities to erect a grain elevator in the Sand Point area of West Saint John and by 1895, Montreal's Beaver Line was calling at the west side pier. As Canadian Pacific's east side rival, the Intercolonial Railway had not stood idle and allowed CPR to become the port's most prominent railway. Besides establishing their rail terminal at this site east of Upper Cove in the 1860s, the ICR had made major improvements to their operations including extending trackage along Courtenay Bay all the way to Lower Cove's shipping berths.

Eventually, the ICR built a rail trestle across Lower Cove to Water Street and erected a new modern grain elevator to compete with CP's west side operations at Reed's Point. And well before the port of Halifax became active in the grain exporting business, Saint John could boast a number of grain elevators on both sides of the harbour. And by the late 1920s, port capacity was pegged at 2,225,000 bushels, increasing to 3,500,000 after World War II. However today, none of the elevators remain on the Saint John waterfront.

ICR Station and Manager's Residence, Moncton, c1905

This photograph is looking east with the train station in the upper right and the Windsor Hotel in the background at the corner of Main and Foundry Streets. This building was swept away in the early 1960s to make way for the High-field Square Shopping Centre. When this photograph was taken, Pictou native David Pottinger was superintendent and general manager of the Intercolonial Railway after replacing C.J. Brydges in 1879. Mr. Pottinger lived comfortably at this opulent Main Street residence. He had been appointed manager of the public railway by Ottawa and ran the ICR as if it were his kingdom. By the 1900s, an elaborate patronage scheme affected most operations of the ICR, and David Pottinger was at the centre of this highly political system that involved purchasing as well as the hiring and firing of railway staff.

Once the Conservative government of Robert Borden came to power in 1911, David Pottinger's days were numbered. In 1913, Pottinger was forced into retirement and a new railway man, American G.P. Gutelius, succeeded Pottinger as general manger and moved into this residence. A contentious four-year period ensued as the ICR was merged with all publicly owned railways in eastern Canada into the Canadian Government Railways, the forerunner to Canadian National Railway. Mr. Gutelius was also a contentious figure, a Conservative manager in a Liberal railway city. He had installed a hothouse where railway employees grew beautiful flowers to decorate railway stations and dining cars. He fought with Moncton Liberal newspaperman John T. Hawke over numerous issues including building the railway subway over Main Street. But publisher Hawke may have gotten the last laugh when he was able to reveal to newspaper readers that Gutelius's salary had been increased from $7000 to $20,000 a year, a remarkable sum for a public servant in Canada during the early 1900s. In 1917, G.P. Gutelius was replaced by C.A. Hayes. In 1918, the Canadian Government Railways became the Canadian National Railway and Hayes remained regional manager until 1923 when L.S. Brown replaced him for one year. In 1924, Ottawa hired W.U. Appleton to be the general manager of the Atlantic region of the Canadian National Railway. Appleton lasted almost twenty years and retired in 1943.

Intercolonial General Offices, Moncton, c1914

Quickly constructed after the 1906 fire, the Intercolonial Railway offices were located on Main Street near the railway station and provided the management and administrative support for the entire ICR system, the only major Canadian railway with its headquarters in the Maritimes. The ICR, with its federal dollars, provided substantial employment to Monctonians but was often accused of dispensing political favours to well-connected citizens. Its monopoly on certain railway services in eastern Canada was a highly political feat that ultimately could not be maintained. When this photo was taken at the beginning of World War I, the new Canadian Government Railways had been formed and now included the National Transcontinental Railway that had reached Moncton in 1913. Eventually all publicly owned railways would be merged and these offices would be maintained as the eastern Canadian administration centre for Canadian National. The building was demolished in 1962 to make way for Highfield Square but the CNR remained Moncton's largest employer well into the 1990s despite reducing its workforce from a high of nearly 5000 in 1970 to less than 500 by 2000. A new eight-story terminal building, nicknamed the "glass house" by Monctonians, was erected directly west of this structure in the early 1960s, serving CN until 2003 when all remaining employees were transferred outside the city to the new Gordon Yard.

Fire at the ICR Shops, Moncton, 1906

In the early 1900s, Moncton was a one-industry city with 2000 people employed at the Intercolonial Railway out of a total population of just over 10,000. The ICR was now the single largest employer in New Brunswick and fear for the future quickly spread throughout Moncton on February 24, 1906, when a fire broke out in the ICR paint shop. Despite a bucket brigade, firefighters were unable to halt the blaze and the fire burned out of control for almost three hours. The burn destroyed the paint shop, boiler-making shop, machine shop, numerous box cars, and other equipment. A number of freight cars were loaded with coal and burned throughout the night. Incoming trains were re-routed or stopped while the fourteen locomotives on site were steamed up and moved to safety. The roundhouses were left standing, as well as the station and offices, but only one of the original working buildings from the 1870s remained—the brick blacksmith shop. Only one employee lost his life. Abram Jones attempted to re-enter the paint shop in order to retrieve a cash box and perished in the flames. The next morning revealed over six acres of destruction and damages in excess of one million dollars. And the city's principal industry lay in ruin. Rumours quickly spread throughout the city that the repair shops would no doubt be rebuilt at a more central location—Halifax or Montreal. Yet fortunately for Moncton, the federal Minister of Railways and Canals was Dorchester lawyer Henry Robert Emmerson.

The former New Brunswick Premier and now federal liberal M. P. for Westmorland was one of Canada's most powerful ministers. And he was determined to see the rebuilding undertaken immediately. His telegram to Monctonians was posted outside the Transcript building on Main Street and read: "Cannot find the words to express my deep regrets, which amounts to sorrow, at a very great disaster which comes so inopportunely, but we must not despair... The Intercolonial will yet triumph. Temporary shops immediately necessary to be followed by more complete and convenient works." Good to his word, Emmerson had temporary shops installed immediately and repair work resumed within a few days. However, the old twenty-five acre site that had served the ICR for thirty years was deemed too small for 20th century railway needs, and within two months, a new site extending over a mile in length was chosen in the city's west end off John Street. Tenders were quickly called to have the repair freight facility rebuilt and the first sod was turned on July 5th.

ICR Fire, Moncton, February 24, 1906

Machine Shops, Intercolonial Railway, Moncton, c1910

This picture shows the new machine and car repair shops built in 1908 away from the downtown railway station off Pacific Avenue in the city's west end. Trains in need of repair would pass over the west subway at Main Street and then again under the bridge at St. George Street before arriving at the new shops. Much of the work was tendered to the then largest rail car manufacturer in Canada, Rhodes, Curry Company of Amherst. Rhodes, Curry also constructed numerous other railway shops and stations throughout the Maritimes. By the fall of 1908, railway workers began to move into the new freight car repair shop facilities that were considered highly mechanized for the time. The expanded facility was known by Monctonians as the "new shops" and could repair sixteen passenger cars at once. And in its heyday prior to the Great Depression, it was one of the most modern railway repairs car shops in North America, employing around 1000 men. Today the entire old ICR repair complex next to Vaughan Harvey Boulevard is gone.

Pullman Car Interior, c1910

The first passenger sleeping car in Canada was built in Hamilton in 1857 and featured double-decker bunks as well as a pot-belly stove for winter travel. But the king of luxury passenger railway cars was the Pullman. Pullman sleeping cars were used extensively on the Intercolonial Railway that ran from Montreal to Rivière-du-Loup, and on to Halifax overnight. On the maiden voyage of the Intercolonial Railway from Halifax on July 3, 1876, Sir Leonard Tilley was one of dignities aboard the train and slept in a Pullman car that was called "Brydges' Palace" by the press. Charles Brydges was the first superintendent of the federal government's railways including the ICR.

In this photograph, the Pullman car has been configured for day-time coach seating but in the evening, porters would drop the sleeping bunks and the car would quickly be converted into a full sleeping unit. The lower seats could also be folded into sleeping berths. The Pullman railway lounge, dinning, and sleeping cars were named after the American inventor of luxury train travel, George M Pullman. He formed the Pullman Palace Car Co. in 1867, and built and serviced sleeping and dining train cars throughout North America and the United Kingdom. Passengers could pay extra and receive additional services such as drinks, refreshments, as well as full meals, and for long distances, overnight sleeping cars were developed by the Pullman Company in the 1880s.

The Pullman Brotherhood of Sleeping Car Porters became an important African-American union in the early 1900s. A large company town called Pullman was developed outside Chicago that included nearly 6,000 employees living and working within the town. The original Pullman manufacturing plant remained in operation at this site until 1955. The company also built thousands of streetcars and trolley cars that they exported worldwide and during the 1920s, various Pullman companies employed over 28,000 people throughout the globe. The Pullman Company purchased their competitor Standard Steel Car Company in 1929 but in the 1940s, the American government filed an anti-trust action against the company forcing it to break up the manufacturing and operating divisions.

Railway Workers Parade, Main Street, Moncton, c1905

Two horses pull the Intercolonial Railway Machinist float during the annual Trades Parade on a rainy afternoon in downtown Moncton. At this time, railways employees in clerical, station, freight, stores, roundhouse, sleeping, and dining car services were members of the International Brotherhood of Railroad Employees with headquarters in Boston. Like most international organizations with a far-flung membership, the IBRE was far removed from local issues and the dissatisfaction surfaced in 1908 when an ICR freight shed foreman, Frank Smith, invited all local divisions of the ICR Brotherhood to meet in Moncton to discuss the prospects of forming an all-Canadian railway worker's union. Delegates from all ICR locals met on October 11, 1908, and voted to withdraw from the International Brotherhood and form an all-Canadian union. The following year, in August 1909, the first Canadian railway labour convention was held in Moncton and the Canadian Brotherhood of Railroad Employees was born.

The Subway, Moncton, c1918

"...Nothing could be more disastrous to the business on Main Street as people would by-pass the subway and use Queen and Victoria Streets. A solution to this could be to have the ICR spend money to rearrange its freight house so as to abolish shunting over Main Street, instead of spending it on this public nuisance." With this hard-hitting editorial in the Moncton Transcript, publisher John T. Hawke launched his attack on Moncton's most debatable question of 1912: whether or not to build a subway with railway tracks over Main Street. Relocation of train tracks in downtown Moncton had been hotly debated for a decade since railways were running at their peak, causing congestion at city intersections and cross-roads. Besides the Intercolonial, the newly built National Transcontinental Railway crossed the Main Street thoroughfare so four tracks intersected Main Street and the rail traffic including Moncton's newly installed street railway system was causing bottle-necks at peak hours.

Railway officials, including Intercolonial boss G.P. Gutelius, favoured con-structing a subway with railway lines passing overtop of Main Street with street traffic, including the brand new streetcars, passing underneath. City officials were divided over whether to agree with the railway's proposal for an overhead pass way, have the lines buried under Main Street, or insist on the lines being diverted away from Main Street. Publisher Hawke wanted the railway lines to come in along Hall's Creek and cross Main Street at its eastern end and then hook up with the old wharf track along the waterfront. In the end, the subway issue was decided by a plebiscite with the voters opting for a subway and excavation began prior to World War I. Main Street was dug with a new invention, the steam-shovel, and this new-fangled outfit created a great attraction for citizens interested in modern high-powered equipment.

Despite major cost-overruns, Moncton's most familiar landmark was completed in 1916 at a cost of $500,000 and after the subway overpass was finished, trains could cross over Main Street without any wait or inconvenience to street traffic. Main Street was also paved at the same time with six inches of concrete base. To try and accommodate the heavy horses that still hauled freight up Main Street to the railway station, wooden blocks were set in asphalt along the hill so that horses could get traction. These strange wooden blocks remained a fixture on "subway hill" until the old horse and wagons were phased out of downtown in the 1930s.

ICR North

ICR Bridge Construction, Southwest Miramichi, 1872

This picture shows a large wooden caisson being prepared for floating into place and then sunk to the bottom of river to help anchor the stonework for the bridge piers. A diver can be seen on the left and his job would have been working the hand-operated dredges and steam pumps that removed water and silt underwater. The mighty Miramichi was certainly one of the largest rivers to require a bridge crossing when the Intercolonial Railway was built by Sir Sanford Fleming in the 1870s. In crossing the Miramichi, Fleming decided to build two smaller bridges over the Southwest and Northwest branches instead of attempting a single large bridge further downriver. However, the bedrock of the two branches turned out to be distinct and the Northwest proved most challenging for installing stable pier footings. On the Southwest, the bedrock below the riverbed proved to be a mixture of hard clay and compact gravel. A caisson was dropped to the riverbed and once the debris was removed, concrete was poured into the gravel to support the foundation stonework that anchored the pier. Once a pier was finished, the caisson was disassembled and moved to a new location where the procedure was repeated until all the piers were in place. Then the bridge could be constructed overtop. This occurred without incident but on the Northwest, establishing a firm foundation for the stonework proved difficult. The problem was a lack of hard clay that supported the gravel on the Southwest.

Silt was the problem around the gravel and each time concrete was poured in to the bottom of the caisson, the foundation would remain unstable and sink. After two years of frustration where the concrete had not set properly, Fleming thought he had the problem solved in the spring of 1874. Yet by late June, the foundation had sunk another six inches. They had already begun work on a number of the piers and over the summer, Fleming's chief engineer began piling hundreds of tons of extra stone and rails on the unfinished piers. And while the foundation did continue to sink throughout the fall, the following spring the foundation had firmed up. Tests revealed that the piers were now secure, and the Northwest Bridge was finally completed in August, 1875, four years after construction had begun.

Northwest Miramichi Railway Bridge, c1890

This six-pier steel bridge was completed in 1875 with each span extending 200 feet in length. This was the last major bridge built in New Brunswick to finish the Intercolonial Railway between Halifax and Rivière-du-Loup. The ICR was officially opened on July 1, 1876, nine years after the terms of Confederation had promised a government constructed railway linking the four British North American colonies. The Intercolonial project had been a huge enterprise for the 1870s but one necessary for a confederation of political union. But it was also a political railway much more than an economic business since it had been constructed along New Brunswick's remote north shore, a condition imposed on the Dominion government by a British fear that a railway constructed along the more heavily populated St John River Valley would be attacked by a hostile United States.

Britain was willing to pay much of the construction costs in order to encourage the union of British North America and despite the massive undertaking, plus patronage issues, and backroom political dealings clouding every aspect of construction, Sir Sanford Fleming managed to build the ICR largely within budget. Prior to Confederation, Fleming had estimated the line would cost approximately $43,348 per mile and his final total including rolling stock, equipment, and spur lines, was $43,180 per mile or just over 21.5 million. In his final report to the prime minister, Sir Sanford Fleming made the following remarks about the completion of Canada's first publicly constructed railway: "The Intercolonial Railway owes its existence to the creation of the Dominion, although it could be said that neither could have been consummated without the other... It is the railway which brings the Maritime Provinces into connection with Central Canada."

Railway Bridge, Southwest Miramichi, c1890

This photograph shows the Miramichi River full of logs moving downstream. This brige was one of the two steel twin bridges over the Miramichi that proved challenging to railway engineers. And one of Sir Sanford Fleming's more remarkable feats as chief engineer and builder of the Intercolonial Railway was convincing the Dominion government, against the wishes of the railway commissioners, to build the bridges using iron and steel instead of wood. Fleming managed to install steel rails instead of iron and converted the line to standard gauge from broad gauge in 1875. Yet his lasting construction contribution was building solid and durable railway bridges. It did not happen without a battle. From the outset, Fleming was adamant that all bridges would be built of iron or would not last. The railway commissioners were equally adamant that iron was too expensive and not necessary.

In 1869, the commissioners offered to compromise and allow five bridges to be built of iron but Fleming appealed directly to the Prime Minister. The Privy Council heard the matter. Commissioner Charles Brydges, also in charge of the Grand Trunk Railway, was most insistent that iron would add another half million in costs to the line and Fleming's concerned that wooden bridges burn easy was nonsense. Fleming was able to provide auditors that backed up his cost estimates, and also pointed out that two Grand Trunk wooden bridges had burned recently. In 1871, a federal order-in-council declared that all ICR bridges constructed henceforward would feature iron superstructures.

ICR Steam Locomotive, Miramichi, c1895

This old steam locomotive No.22 features the common American wheel arrangement (4-4-0) and may have been sitting on a short spur line waiting for a freighter to pass. Steam power slowly began to replace water, wind, and horse power before 1800, but high pressure steam engines capable of generating up to one hundred horsepower were not introduced into British and American industries until around 1805. By the 1820s, steam power—steam under pressure, began driving many of the stationary sawmills in North America and steamboats also began appearing in coastal waters. The next decade saw the beginning of steam locomotion whereby boiling water turned iron wheels on trains through an elaborate system of valves, pistons, cylinders, levers, and rods.

This rolling stock—steam that generated motion, was revolutionary in a way that few people can appreciate today since mechanical travel is now so common and part of our everyday lives. And until Confederation, experimental locomotives were turned out in great fashion featuring enlarged or double boilers, strange fireboxes, and many other early designs. The basic requirements were quite simple, and other than the necessary cowcatcher on the front, driving wheels, boiler, firebox, and smokestack, an early locomotive could be built in many different ways. By the 1870s, much of the design of the steam locomotive became fixed but its wheel arrangement continued to change from the light Mogul (2-6-0 wheel assembly meaning a single axle in front with 2 wheels and 3 axles in the middle with 6 wheels) to the Atlantic (4-4-2). Finally, the largest steam locomotive, the uniquely Canadian-made Northern, came on steam with its 16 wheels (4-8-4) and heavy, all-weather engine. Driving wheel diameters also varied from earlier sizes of 50" to around 84" on the Atlantic type locomotive. The American wheel arrangement (4-4-0) was certainly the most common steam locomotive throughout railway history and for a time, Canadian Pacific had around 400 of these locomotives in operation. Ten-wheeler locomotives (4-6-0) were also very popular. At least ten different locomotive designs were constructed throughout Canada including the famous *Loostack* and *Ossekeag* engines at the Phoenix Foundry in Saint John.

ICR Station, Derby Junction, Miramichi River in the Background, c1887

Derby Junction served as the mainland point between the two railway bridges that crossed the Northwest and Southwest Miramichi Rivers. After a spur line for lumber products was constructed 13 miles west to Indiantown, Derby Station served the ICR as the inter-connector that linked the north-south ICR line between Moncton and Quebec with the spur line that followed the Southwest Miramichi past Millerton to Quarryville and Indiantown (Renous.) This junction was also the crossing point for the Canada Eastern Railway to Fredericton. In the late 1800s, the ICR competed with the Canada Eastern Railway that ran from Chatham to Fredericton. In 1894, the Canada Eastern line extended its tracks five miles upriver past Chatham to Loggieville and had yearly figures of well over 10,000 tons in freight and 40,000 passengers. But after 1900, the Canada Eastern Railway struggled with competition from the ICR and eventually, the ICR became the owner and operator of Canada Eastern.

Railway Crash on the ICR, Newcastle, c1895

This Ole Larsen photo shows a number of freight cars destroyed as well as torn tracks and a damaged locomotive among the wreck. A second train sits idle on the left. While it remains uncertain what train wreck this picture has captured, Michael Nowlan in his book, *Ole Larsen's Miramichi*, has confirmed that the picture was indeed taken near the Newcastle train station. The two houses on the right are still standing and author Nowlan has also identified in the background on the right, the tiny turret of the Roman Catholic Church in Newcastle. While Nowlan also points out that this photo is too early to be connected with the terrible crash near Beaverbrook Station in 1907, many train wrecks during the late 1800s did occur near stations since additional train traffic would be present and communication between the station and the moving train was still in its infancy.

Loading Spool Wood, Bartibog, c1895

Once railways were built they ran deep through the New Brunswick wilderness and offered opportunities for lumbermen to harvest wood in places that were previously inaccessible. Bartibog above the Miramichi River was one such area where few logging roads had penetrated into the pristine woods when the Intercolonial Railway opened for business in 1876. Harvesting the forests along the rail line was then made possible, and in the 1880s and 1890s, spool wood became in high demand overseas. Spools for threads were made from hardwood until the 1960s and Britain's textile mills were humming when this Ole Larsen photo was taken in the late 1890s. Yellow birch made the best spool wood and Bartibog's vast hardwood stands were well known to lumbermen.

As this picture shows, lumbermen would cut the birch into straight, four-foot lengths and ship the timber by rail to Newcastle where the Corry Clarke mill produced tens of thousands of spools on contract for the J.P. Coates Company of Glasgow, Scotland. Finished spool wood became an important export for the province and while the Corry Clarke mill went out of production in the early 1900s, other mills in New Brunswick continue to produce and export spool wood to the UK and New England until the middle of the 20th century.

ICR Passenger Train, Bathurst, c1890

Although no longer standing, the old ICR station at Bathurst became famous in 1914 not for its stunning architectural details but for unwittingly hosting a dramatic gunfight between authorities and Bathurst's own notorious Billy the Kid. William Gagnier was a desperate criminal who had earned local notoriety for numerous armed robberies. Gagnier managed to break out of the Gloucester County Jail one April evening in 1914 and the next morning, authorities discovered that the W. J. Kent Store had been robbed of jewellery and a number of revolvers were also missing. A manhunt was quickly ordered and a posse combed the streets of Bathurst. That night, Deputy Sheriff Doucett arrived at the ICR station after receiving reports of a stranger lurking in one of the railway cars. Searching the cars with his flashlight, he suddenly came upon the escaped convict William Gagnier who had two revolvers pointed directly at him.

A gunfight erupted and one of Gagnier's revolvers was shot out of his hand. The shoot-out continued as William Gagnier ran down the tracks firing at the pursing Sheriff Doucett. The running gunfight turned desperate as Gagnier's wounded hand and loss of blood left him weak and cornered against a high wire fence. Yet Gagnier continued to fire from his one good hand until he ran out of cartridges. Sheriff Doucett was then able to unarm his prisoner and drag him back to the station. Very shortly, the infamous criminal was once again placed in the county jail and guarded around the clock.

ICR Railway Station at Jacquet River, c1900

Jacquet River lies about thirty miles above Bathurst and Charlo is situated another fifteen miles north. On October 9, 1909, the ICR *Freight Special* No 33 rushed out of Bathurst almost forty minutes late. Engineer John Morton had mentioned to his colleagues at Bathurst that he would try and make up the time by Jacquet River or Charlo for sure. Firing up the engine, the No 33 began speeding north. A bit later at Charlo, the *Maritime Express* No.32 was also running late after delays taking on water. Engineer Robert Whalen assured fireman Herman Smith that they could make up the missing time by Bathurst if they hurried. Fireman Smith stoked up the big steam engine as they sped south.

Something terrible happened that day and a sequent inquiry was inconclusive but it's certain that a communication failure resulted in three deaths. *Freight Special* No 33 got to Jacquet River first but apparently engineer Morton was in a hurry, and was waved through the station without being switched over or informed that the *Maritime Express*, running late out of Charlo, was bearing down on Jacquet River full throttle. Both trains were running wide out and unfortunately towards each other north of Jacquet River when fireman Herman Smith looked up and cried: "My God, 33 is on us!" Smith jumped out of the engine and landed in a ditch while the two trains crashed. Smith remembered the terrible sound of the two engines crashing while he was still in the air. While he lived to tell his story, both engineers and a second crewmember of No.33 died in the dreadful train wreck.

Intercolonial Railway Tunnel at Morrisey Rock, c1875

While constructing the Intercolonial from Rivière-du-Loup through to Halifax involved moving massive amounts of earth including over one and a half million cubic yards of rock, the only tunnel necessary was through the Morrisey Rock just west of Campbellton. The bore measured a modest 166 feet and was one of the easier tasks along the route since rock cutting in total along the ICR extended for over six miles, and was especially difficult in the Bathurst area. This section of the ICR between Campbellton and Ste. Flave (Mont Joli) was the last to be completed. It opened in the late spring of 1876 while the Moncton to Campbellton section was finished in 1875.

The Moncton to Truro stretch had opened in 1872 while the Truro to Halifax line had been completed back in 1858 as part of the original Nova Scotia Railway. On the other side, Rivière-du-Loup through to Quebec City had been constructed in the 1860s as part of the Grand Trunk Railway. Truro though to Rivière-du-Loup measured 500 miles and then a number of branch lines were added immediately to the ICR inventory of railways as well as the European and North American Railway from the Maine-New Brunswick border to Pointe-du-Chêne. And when it officially opened on July 1, 1876, the Dominion government's Intercolonial Railway owned and operated extensive railways throughout

New Brunswick and Nova Scotia. And almost immediately, the ICR began adding new railways as locally owned lines began to lose money and threatened to close down unless the government agreed to take them over. By World War I, the ICR operated over 2000 miles of tracks throughout the region and in the 1930s, virtually all railways in the Maritimes were owned and operated by the Dominion government's CNR or the Canadian Pacific.

Waiting for the Train, Intercolonial Railway Station, Campbellton, c1910

This beautiful and somewhat elaborate train station was built in the 1870s and included many features that may have seemed extravagant for the needs of a town of only 600 people. But in many ways, the ICR had correctly predicted the future and realized that many new and vital community functions would be needed as the railway station soon became the central meeting point for a railway town in the late 1800s. In addition to waiting rooms and ticket station, the Campbellton station featured a cashier's office, a bank, superintendent and engineer's offices as well as a station master's apartment. And business was brisk at Campbellton when the railway opened in 1876. Train goers came into the community from all over northern New Brunswick to catch the train going west to Montreal or south to Moncton and Halifax. In addition, Campbellton served as the turn-around site for railway crews coming out of Moncton.

ICR Branch Lines

First Passenger Train at Dalhousie, June 25, 1884

This photo shows a man standing with children on the cowcatcher while other members of the crew are inside and on the side of the No.118 ICR locomotive. The Dalhousie Branch Railway Company was formed in 1873 in order to build a branch line to connect Dalhousie with the Intercolonial Railway. The ICR had been announced to proceed south from Campbellton but would bypass the community. No sooner had the Intercolonial Railway began speeding through New Brunswick, delivering passengers and freight into Upper Canada and back south to Nova Scotia, when towns and villages not situated on the railway line began lobbying to have spur lines built into their communities. Convincing railway officials of the business case to build connecting lines was one thing but the Intercolonial was not really an economic animal but a political railway. Lobbying federal politicians to help build connecting lines became an important activity and one of the first to succeed was Dalhousie. Within a decade, many branch lines were owned and operated by the ICR and while they had been extended far beyond their original borders, these feeder lines brought substantial numbers of passengers and freight into the main ICR line. And by 1900, virtually every significant community in New Brunswick had access to a railway line.

International Railway Station, St. Léonard, c1910

This photo shows the local stationmaster outside the station with a sign overhead indicating the station also served as a telegraph office. For twenty-five years, a rail line from Campbellton to the St. John River slowly took shape across some of the province's most rugged and wild terrain. But once completed, the line was then forced to struggle again to stay in business. In 1885, the Restigouche and Victoria Colonization Railway Company was incorporated with a business plan to build a line 100 miles to Grand Falls. The company failed to raise the construction funds and so in 1897, a new company called the Restigouche and Western Railway Company formed with a plan to build a more modest route through to St. Leonard and connect with the New Brunswick Railway.

The company raised $800,000 and began construction but the terrain was so tough that after four years, the company had only managed to build eleven miles out of Campbellton. Even after the federal government offered to double the subsidy in places where the company could demonstrate rough geography, progress was slow. In 1906, a new company called the International Railway Company became the principal builder, managing to sell some of the company stock to the provincial government in exchange for cash. Finally in 1910, the line opened measuring a total of 110 miles and met the NTR and CPR lines at St. Leonard. But the line immediately struggled to operate without incurring huge losses. Even a new bridge over the St. John River to Maine, allowing the line to connect with the Bangor and Aroostook Railway, failed to create a profit for the operators. In 1914, the federal government purchased the line for just under $3,000,000 and then in 1919, the CNR became the owner and operator of the railway. By the late 1980s, CNR had virtually abandoned the old IRC.

No. 33 Train With Passengers and Freight, Caraquet Railway, c1896

In 1874, the Caraquet Railway Company was formed but it took another ten years before construction would start on a line that had been surveyed from the ICR main line at Gloucester Junction to Shippagan, a distance of 66 miles. The promoters claimed to have raised almost one million dollars and another $300,000 in government subsides but it took another decade to build the line across a sparsely populated area comprised of difficult terrain that included solid rock mixed with peat bogs. Finally in 1895, the line had reached Stonehaven and was then extended another 25 miles to Upper Caraquet. The 14-mile stretch to Pokemouche Junction was completed in 1897 and finally in 1898, the railway was built through to Shippagan. Once finished, the Caraquet Railway limped along with limited freight and passenger traffic, breaking even once or twice but generally reporting losses each year. In 1911, the railway merged with the Gulf Shore Railway Company that had been built from Pokemouche Junction south to Tracadie-Sheila. The new railway was called the Caraquet and Gulf Shore Railway but making money still remained a problem. In 1918, the federal government was buying and amalgamating railways, and offered the owners $200,000 lock, stock, and barrel. Yet the owners wanted more. Negations took place but in 1920, the Dominion government indicated that $200,000 was their final offer and of course, the offer was then accepted as the money-losing line was rolled into the Canadian Government Railways that became part of the Canadian National Railway system in the 1920s. In the 1980s and 1990s, the remaining portions of the Caraquet and Gulf Shore Railway were finally abandoned.

Shippegan Railway Station, Caraquet and Gulf Shore Railway, c1911

By the 1930s, the old Caraquet and Gulf Shore Railway had been owned and operated by Canadian National for two decades. Bathurst through to Tracadie was normally a day's journey even in the dead of winter. Yet one winter's day in 1935, CN's *Caraquet Flyer* left Bathurst for Tracadie and took five days to arrive. A huge snowstorm hit the morning the train left the station and since snowdrifts were already heavy along the line due to previous storms, CN had already hired numerous snow shovellers to accompany the train. But the drifts were so high—

twelve feet drifts were not uncommon—that shovellers had to clear out the telegraphy lines as well. Levees were built to allow men to shovel in layers one to the other, and up to four men shovelling on four levels were required to get to the top of some drifts. At one point, up to one hundred shovellers were working in front of the train attempting to clear a path. Yet on the second day, after twelve hours of shovelling, the train had only advanced a half mile. Water became in short supply and snow was melted to use in the coal-fired steam engines. CN paid each shoveller two dollars per eight-hour shift and workers were happy for the back-breaking work in the depressed 1930s. Finally, on the fourth day, winds came up, blowing drifts away from the tracks, and the *Caraquet Flyer* limped into Tracadie on the morning of the fifth day.

Train With Men Clearing Snow, Kent County, c1915

When the Intercolonial Railway trunk line between Quebec and Halifax was completed in 1876, branch lines connecting into the ICR became popular with New Brunswickers. And the New Brunswick Legislature offered significant subsidies for every mile of track that was built regardless of where the tracks would be laid. This ensured the appearance of the slick railway promoter—operators that were willing to build railroads but not operate them. In Kent County, the ICR ran north-south and the citizens of the coastal area around Richibucto were interested in a branch line running inland to the ICR, a distance of 26 miles. In 1881, after raising $60,000 in stock and a promise of $5,000 a mile provincial government subsidy, as well as $3,200 a mile in federal assistance, construction started. A municipal grant and further stock offering allowed the line to open in 1883, and the Kent Northern Railway Company managed to stay in the black for six years, mainly hauling gravel into the ICR station at Kent Junction. However in 1890, the company defaulted on a loan payment and the Imperial Trust Company took over the line. Throughout the 1890s, the line sputtered along but was unable to pay its debt. In 1903, the railway was reorganized with hopes of selling the Kent Northern to new investors but nothing materialized except controversy when it was discovered that the increased freight numbers spurring the pending sales had been apparently rigged. A group based in Toronto took over the line in 1911 and freight numbers did jump during World War I. In 1929, CNR purchased the Northern Kent Railway Company for $60,000 and continued to operate the branch line until abandoning the entire railway in 1989.

Moncton & Bouctouche Railway Tracks, Marven's Factory, Moncton, 1931

This photo is looking east from the air with Hall's Creek in the background. Moncton's old Cotton Mill is now home to Marven's and is visible in the middle of the photo. Factory Lane off King Street leads from the bottom of the photo directly to the tower where a company sign is still visible. Directly behind the building is the factory's water pond, and to the right of the smokestack is a rail spur line for shipping and receiving that led across Main Street and along the waterfront to the main CN trunk line near Eaton's. The last stop of the old Moncton & Bouctouche Railway is visible in the upper right but by the 1930s, the rail line had moved over to the Union Station near the subway. The railway bridge across Hall's Creek is also gone and the M & B railway used the main CN line to exit and enter the city. Harper's Lane runs along the right edge of the photo. Established in 1886 as the Bouctouche and Moncton Railway, the little 32-mile rail line was known locally as the B & M railway and then later was reorganized as the Moncton and Bouctouche Railway. A Moncton newspaper reported the following in August, 1886: "The Annual Meeting of the B & M. Railway Co. was held in the Scotch Settlement School. The report of Mr. Killam, manager, was very encouraging. C. P. Harris was elected President. Rev. J. D. Murray, Secy. A Board of Directors was also elected. Nov. 16, 1887: The Bouctouche and Moncton Railway ballasting is almost completed. Trains are expected to run over the completed Route by December. John N. Brown, contractor for the Moncton Station has commenced operations. April 29, 1888."

Once established, the B & M suffered from a shortage of adequate traffic in order to ensure its continued operation. Placed in the hands of the Sheriff and sold to American interests in 1891, the line continued to operate as a mail, cargo, and passenger service from downtown Moncton northeast through Lewisville, Irishtown, Tankville, Cape Breton, Scotch Settlement, MacDougall, Notre-Dame, St. Anthony, and McKees Mill, before finally arriving at Bouctouche. In 1918, the federal government purchased the line for $70,000 and merged it into the CN system. After World War 11, passenger service was eliminated and the line was finally abandoned in 1965.

Train Crash on the M & B, February 20, 1914

Within the span of six months, two major train crashes occurred in Westmorland County and these wrecks are still remembered today as two of the worst railway accidents in Atlantic Canada. On September 24, 1913, a head-on crash on the main ICR trunk line outside Aulac resulted in the death of five men and shortly thereafter, a terrible wreck on the Moncton and Bouctouche Railway at Scotch Settlement plunged the entire operation of the branch line into question. In February 1914, the snowfall had been especially heavy and trains on the M & B were having difficulty getting through the drifts. On the 20th, the snow clearing train was dispatched from Moncton and aboard one of the two locomotives was the line's Superintendent Frank Hall. At 3:00 P.M., the snow train suddenly crashed through a tall, frozen wooden trestle near Scotch Settlement. Two locomotives, the snow plow, and two box cars plunged into the frozen ground below killing Frank Hall and a number of other railway employees.

The shocked citizens of New Brunswick awoke the next morning to see the front page of the Moncton Transcript ablaze with news of another terrible train tragedy: "TRAIN GOES THROUGH BRIDGE ON M. & B. RAILWAY AT SCOTCH SETTLEMENT; FOUR MEN KILLED" Besides Frank Hall, driver Gideon Smith, fireman George Freeman, along with brakeman Sylvang Bourque, were all instantly killed from the crash. As well, five men were injured including three workers with broken bones. Later that week, a double funeral at Bouctouche saw an enormous assembly pay their last respects to local railway engineer Smith and fireman Freeman. The feeble wooden bridge had collapsed like glass unable to hold the two-engine train along with the heavy snow and ice that had collected over the previous week. A coroner's inquest into the wreck later ruled that an ice flow in the stream below had struck and moved some of the trestle supports causing the bridge to fall in under the strain. At the inquest, Bouctouche engineer Alex McKie recalled driving one of the locomotives and as the bridge collapsed he yelled, "we are all going to be killed." The next thing he remembered was being carried away from the wreck and arriving at the Moncton Hospital. While the coroner's jury did not lay blame on anyone for the mishap, they did recommend that guardrails be attached to all bridges along the M & B railway.

While an ICR relief train was called in to clear the track, the M & B railway was still an independent railway in 1914, and its limited resources meant that regular traffic did not resume until March. The big crash was not the only accident that caused loss of life on the M & B line—another brakeman, Jude White, was killed in a shunting accident along the line at Cape Breton. However, the 1914 mishap was clearly the worst train wreck on the branch line and no doubt hasten the branch line's financial difficulties in maintaining operations. The engines and tracks were eventually repaired and the wooden trestle rebuilt, but the branch line struggled even further during World War 1.

Building the Ferry Terminal at Borden, PEI, c1915

With Prince Edward Island joining Confederation in 1873, regular ferry service commenced between the island to Shediac and Pictou. But in 1883, a group of businessmen in Sackville began to build a branch rail line to Cape Tormentine. The first 18 miles to Baie Verte were finished the same year and the full 36 miles to Cape Tormentine was completed in 1886. The railway became known as the New Brunswick and Prince Edward Island Railway Company and since the terrain was relatively flat with few streams to cross, and no great need for expensive ballast, the construction was finished for less than $7,000 per mile. This left the builders a hefty profit when all the railway construction subsides were added up.

The rails and other equipment were all cheap ICR rejects, and the enterprising Sackville group also managed to record an operating surplus most years. Many influential Westmorland businessmen had invested in the Cape Tormentine Railway project including Sackville entrepreneur Josiah Wood, Acadian lawyer Pierre A. Landry (later Chief Justice), and Albert County railway builder, Amasa Killam. The Cape Tormentine Railway was a rarity in 19th century New Brunswick since construction costs did not greatly exceed the government subsidy. ICR statistics revealed that the total federal and provincial subsidy totalled $212,709, or $5,909 per mile while total construction costs only exceeded the subsidy by $60,000. A bond issued for $100,000 covered the remaining costs and still left some operating funds while a stock issue for $214,850 was fully sub-scribed, leaving the principal owners showing a tidy profit before the first train left the Sackville ICR station. The Cape Tormentine Railway quickly gained the lion's share of freight shipments to PEI as it offered fast and reliable con-nections with the main ICR line to Upper Canada. At the beginning of World War I, the Dominion government purchased the railway outright for a total of $270,000 and after World War I, year-round ferry service was installed from Cape Tormentine to Borden. Canadian National ran the entire service including all rail operations on Prince Edward Island until 1988 when CN was allowed to abandon the line as well as all rail service on the island.

CNR Ferry, Cape Tormentine, 1931

With Prince Edward Island in the far distance, the car and rail ferry is loading for a daily crossing to the island. During World War I, Cape Tormentine became the ferry terminus connecting with the New Brunswick and Prince Edward Island Railway from Sackville. The first crossing of the new daily car ferry service to Cape Traverse began on October 16, 1917 with the sailing of the first truly efficient ice-breaking ferry named Prince Edward Island. The last dangerous crossing of PEI's famous iceboats also took place the same year. The old weekly winter eight and one-half mile iceboat crossing carried both mail and passengers. The iceboats usually comprised a captain, coxswain, and four crewmembers that sailed, rowed, or even dragged the boat over the ice depending on the conditions. Most trips were dangerous and usually involved all three methods of travel. Male passengers could have their fare reduced in half if they agreed to assist in pulling the boat over ice flows. Each hauler was issued a long leather strap that would fit around one's shoulder and waist, also serving as a rescue line if the ice gave out. On a good winter's day, crossing the strait would take about three to four hours but on dirty days, a crossing could take all day and even longer if the boat became struck in the ice. Fog or driving snow could easily confuse an experienced iceboat captain. It was always possible to end up turned around, with the boat travelling in the wrong direction, straight up the strait, parallel to the mainland. In 1843, ten people attempting to cross the strait remained lost on the ice for two days. When Prince Edward Island joined Confederation in 1873, one of the conditions of the union with the Dominion of Canada was a guarantee of steamship service all year long between the island and the mainland. It was only with the sailing of this vessel, the Prince Edward Island, that islanders truly felt the Dominion of Canada had finally fulfilled this essential condition of Confederation.

Enterprise Foundry and Sackville Train Station, 1931

Sackville's Enterprise Foundry with the CN railway station on the right and Mount Allison University in the background. Enterprise stoves, ranges, and furnaces were the featured products in 1931 according to the large sign. On the far right stands the CNR Station, built with local red sandstone by ICR chief engineer William MacKenzie (1897-1911). Behind the station and in back of the water tower stands the Sackville Hotel. Sackville's first major hotel was completed in 1889 and proved popular due to the location next to the railway and the town's waterfront. By 1900, the hotel was known as the Intercolonial Hotel, and was destroyed in the big 1907 fire that also destroyed the nearby Enterprise Foundry. Quickly rebuilt, the hotel continued on until about the time this picture was taken. The Depression years were hard on the hotel business since most railway passengers simply slept on the trains. By the late 1930s, the hotel closed and was never reopened. However, the building is still standing today.

Sackville was a railway crossroads and the train station serviced passengers going south to Halifax, east to Prince Edward Island and north to Moncton. A double spur line with a single box car is visible leading into the foundry. Captain R. M. Dixon and a group of local farmers established the Enterprise Foundry in Sackville in 1872 under the business name of Dominion Foundry Company, producing only stoves for the first few years. The ICR railway line was under construction during this period and Captain Dixon picked a site near the railway station but still close enough to the town wharf so that the company could be able to ship their products by rail or water.

Train & Car Accident, Sackville, June 18, 1931

A Saturday afternoon train and car crash at the level crossing in Sackville created pandemonium in the town as a car driven by W. B. Logan crashed into the passenger train coming into the Sackville Railway Station. This photo from almost overhead shows people gathered around the crash scene near Bridge Street and Lorne, as passenger Mamie Driscoll of Legere Corner perished in the accident and three others including the driver of the car were hospitalized. An inquest determined that faulty car brakes caused the collision. One witness at the inquiry, Mrs. Silas LeBlanc of Sackville, stated that the automobile party had stopped at her home before the accident and had complained a number of times that the brakes were not working very well. Testimony by car mechanic Lester Lowther confirmed the defective brake verdict and also agreed with the railway's own investigation that stated no Canadian National employees were at fault. Statements from the engineer and train crew indicated that they were surprised by the sudden appearance of what seemed to be a runaway automobile unable to stop.

Eyewitness reports to New Brunswick Provincial Police investigators expressed the view that after the driver realized he was unable to stop the car, he attempted to steer the automobile parallel to the train in order to avoid the head-on collision. However, W. B. Logan was unable to avoid running into the train and the tragic fatality could have been easily avoided if the car's brakes had been working properly. There were few overpasses in the 1930s and level crossings where train and automobiles met were dangerous sites since high speed crashes almost always meant serious injury or death. Flashing lights, gates, and other warning signs were installed on all CN level crossings by the beginning of World War II, partly as a result of this train-car accident in downtown Sackville. In fact, this level crossing was eventually eliminated as the railway tracks were moved away from crossing over Bridge Street in order to cut down on potential car-train collusions.

Salisbury & Albert Railway, Hillsborough, 1931

Looking northeast along Hillsborough's main street with the Petitcodiac River in the upper right corner. Crossing the road at the bottom are the railway tracks of the gypsum mines that delivered gypsum to a wharf on the Petitcodiac River for waiting steamers to ship the prize mineral to the United States. Also, a significant amount of gypsum was shipped by rail out of Albert County to markets in Canada and the United States. Local gypsum was also used in a plasterboard plant that had been established at nearby Grey's Island. A second set of tracks can be seen crossing the road further north with two CN freight cars and a tanker sitting on a siding. This line belonged to the Salisbury & Albert Railway, built by well-known railway builder and operator Amasa E. Killam.

The Albert Railway Company was organized before Confederation at $10,000 per mile subsidy with the intention of establishing a branch line from Albert Mines and Hillsborough to connect at Salisbury with the European and North American Railway between Saint John and Shediac. Opened in 1876, the line was extended in 1892 to Alma as well as over to Harvey Bank with the lower section known as the Albert Southern Railway. Lumber and coal were hauled but Hillsborough gypsum was the main cargo. The line went through a number of ownership changes until 1918 when the branch became part of the federal CNR system. Like most branch railways in the Maritimes, the line was largely abandoned to commercial traffic in the late 20th century.

Hillsborough Railway Station, c1940

Railway builder and 19th century politician, Amasa Emerson Killam, built and managed the Albert Railway in the early years. A.E. Killam was a colourful character with little formal education. His father had fought for the British in the American Revolution and settled in Dorchester before moving to Salisbury and operating a blacksmith trade. One of ten Killam children, Amasa, lived in Moncton during the 1850s. He settled in Wheaton Settlement in the 1860s where he farmed and operated the local post office. Yet his passion was building bridges and along with partner John Brown, Killam built the second Coverdale Bridge over the Petitcodiac River in 1870 at Moncton, after the 1869 Saxby Gale destroyed the first bridge. In 1872, A.E. Killam received the contract to build a bridge over Halls' Creek connecting Moncton with Leger's Corner (Dieppe).

During this period, the European and North American Railway was operating between Saint John and Pointe-du-Chêne, and passed through Salisbury. Killam reasoned that a railway branch from Salisbury through Hillsborough to

Albert Mines would allow minerals to be shipped to markets south and west through the ENAR. He built the Albert Railway and after it opened in 1876, Killam operated the line for a number of years. But building railways became his major interest and he built the St. Martin's and Upham Railway in 1881, operating the branch line for five years. Killam also built the Petitcodiac and Havelock Railway in 1886, and also managed the line. Like most successful 19th century businessmen, A.E. Killam was also a politician and represented Westmorland County in the provincial legislature for a number of years. He supported John A. Macdonald and his National Policy in Dominion politics and became known as a liberal in the late 1800s. Throughout the 1890s and early years of the 1900s, Killam invested in many business ventures throughout Westmorland County and remained active in railway companies until the First World War.

Cumberland Basin with Old Ship Railway Site, 1931

The abandoned Chignecto Ship Railway can be seen running through this picture from the lower left to the upper right. At the New Brunswick-Nova Scotia border, in the late 19th century, a Fredericton engineer attempted to build a very different kind of railway.

Henry Ketchum grew up in Fredericton and enrolled in civil engineering at King's College in 1854. He worked in railway construction throughout New Brunswick and for a time in Brazil, earning a reputation as a skilful and energetic engineer. In 1865, he was charged with constructing the eastern extension of the European & North American Railway, from Moncton to the Nova Scotia border. While surveying on the Isthmus of Chignecto, Ketchum concocted his vision of the age old dream that would allow ships to cross the Isthmus from the Bay of Fundy to the Northumberland Strait at Baie Verte. Ketchum's idea was to build the first ship railway in the world that would hoist fully loaded vessels, by means of a hydraulic lift, onto double rail tracks where two trains would pull the ship the 27 kilometres to the other shore. The merchants of Saint John would benefit the most from such a shortcut that promised to save up to 800 kilometres shipping between Montreal, Saint John, and Boston.

While the technology was untested, Ketchum felt that a ship railway was superior to a canal since it was cheaper to build and maintain, would allow paddle-wheelers to cross while a canal would not, and would solve the question of a tidal difference between the two bodies of water. In 1882, Ketchum formed the Chignecto Marine Transport Railway Company and was able to raise £650,000 in Britain after the Government of Canada agreed to pay an annual subsidy of $150,000 for twenty-five years. Yet a condition was imposed that the annual subsidy would only be paid once the project was completed. Cumberland County agreed to provide the land at no charge and construction commenced in 1888 with extensive docks being erected at Fort Lawrence near the entrance to LaPlance River, and at Tidnish Bridge on the Northumberland Strait. In 1891, 19 kilometres of track had been laid and three quarters of the entire project completed at a cost of $3,500,000. Yet the remaining $1,500,000 needed to finish the ship railway was not to arrive.

The Canadian government had given additional guarantees but would go no further, and Ketchum's British partners were unable to raise more funds. Despite fierce debates in the House of Commons, construction never resumed after 1891. The wood structures were uprooted and used in nearby farms, and much of the heavy rock was reused to maintain the Intercolonial Railway, and later to build the ferry terminal at Cape Tormentine. Ketchum's pioneering project ultimately failed because of the uncertainty surrounding the amount of ship traffic the crossing would eventually generate. His ability to build the ship railway was not in doubt but his enthusiastic tonnage estimates was considered too optimistic, especially in the early 1890s when Maritime shipping began to decline. Building railways as public works projects went out of fashion by this time, and governments were simply unwilling to risk more public funds. A brilliant and energetic engineer, Henry Ketchum died in Amherst in 1896.

Canadian
National

Sir Henry Thornton, CNR Boss, 1922

By the end of World War 1, Canadian railways had done a good job moving troops and freight in and out of the busy east coast ports, but financially, railways were in trouble. Wartime inflation had increased costs but not railway fees.

Strict national laws had prevented transportation companies and other essential services from increasing their rates. In 1918, the Canadian Government took over the Canadian Northern Railway and the next year, with the pending closure of the Grand Trunk, created the Canadian National Railway, a merger of all government owned railways. The new railway creation was headquartered in Montreal and the old ICR, as an independent Maritime railway, was no more.

By 1922, the restructuring had been complete and the CNR's first President, Sir Henry Thornton, had been installed with the promise that politics would no longer dictate the fate of Canada's railway system. He made the following announcement: "Let it be emphatically understood, now and for once and for all, that there is to be no political interference, direct or indirect, in the administration and workings of the Canadian National Railways... The Prime Minister has solemnly assured that there is to be no political interference, and it was with this distinct understanding that I accepted the post which the Government has done me the honour to offer."

Did politics no longer interfere with railways? No, but throughout the roaring twenties, Canadian National Railway and its 100,000 employees did a good job upgrading their transportation system and managed to compete with the private Canadian Pacific Railway. The old description of the CNR as standing for Collect No Revenues was long forgotten as both national railways had enough passengers and freight to operate profitably. Hotels and railway terminals were built and upgraded, and the CNR under President Thornton introduced a number of innovative services including a radio service that eventually blossomed into the Canadian Broadcasting Corporation. He also managed to maintain good relations with CNR's unionized employees, certainly no easy task. Business was strong until the 1930s when the Great Depression reduced most railways to bare bones operations, and the CNR went into a tailspin only to rise again during World War 11. Unfortunately for Henry Thornton, his presidency have been created and maintained by the Liberal government under MacKenzie King and when Richard Bennett's Conservative Party came to power in 1930, Thornton became the scapegoat for all of Canada's economic ills. Periodically harassed and ignored by Bennett, Thornton resigned in 1932 and died several months later in Montreal.

CN Railway Yard, Moncton, 1931

This view is looking east across the city to Lewisville and Sunny Brae. Eaton's can be seen where Albert Street meets Foundry Street and in the far upper right, the marsh at Hall's Creek is visible. Along the corner of Albert and Foundry Streets, stands Government Row, a row of railway tenement houses that were built in the 19th century to accommodate ICR workers and their families. In fact, most of the homes around Albert Street housed railway workers. Main Street borders the rail yard on the north with the Union Station visible as well as the two CN office buildings further to the left of the picture. Union Station was built in 1897 as the Intercolonial Station, and renamed Union after Canadian National, National Transcontinental Railway, and the Moncton & Bouctouche Railway all began using the station. In the 1960s, part of this area next to Main Street would be transformed into Highfield Square, a downtown shopping centre.

CN Railway Shops, Moncton, May 27, 1931

The new shops built after the 1906 fire with the camera looking northwest from over St George Street. At the bottom right can be seen the end of John Street coming into the shops and Canadian National's parking lot, with perhaps a dozen parked automobiles. Just off the picture at the bottom is the Speedway Race Track and in upper right side of the photo shows undeveloped land that a decade later would become the No. 31 Military Depot. Across the railway tracks on the left runs Pacific Avenue, connecting Killam Drive to St. George Street. Far in the upper left is the future site of Nature Park, renamed Centennial Park in 1967. The railway tracks leading to the shops from the bottom left crossed Main Street twice, at the main subway and then again over the west subway where it continued under the bridge at St. George Street.

After 1963, trains in need of repair could be routed to the shops from the new Hump Yard further west off Edinburgh Drive. This allowed the west Main Street subway and the St. George Street crossing to be removed. Now the Moncton Common, this massive car works was the largest employer in the city from 1908 until the late 1970s. The peak years for employment at the CN Repair Shops were just prior to 1930. After World War I, about 1000 men worked in the shops and during the summer of 1928, an important change at the shops took place. Instead of repairing locomotives, passenger, and freight car exclusively, the CN Repair Shop proudly produced two locomotives that had been fully built at the Moncton shops.

The first engine was No. 8334. Unfortunately, within six months of this picture being taken, and as the Depression economy continued to worsen, deep cuts to the railway worker's hours were made. The Repair Shops ran intermittently during the Depression Era when an average year saw workers only employed fifteen days a month. However, fifteen days a month was still better than most Maritimers could expect to work and virtually no workers left the railway for better working hours elsewhere.

CN Roundhouse, Moncton, October 7, 1931

This photo was taken from the air while over the Petitcodiac River looking towards Lutz Mountain. The building in the centre is Swift Canadian Co. Limited and dozens of pigs are in the pasture at the front of the plant. Behind the building is the large Canadian National Railway's roundhouse with Newton Heights in the background. In the distance on the right are the CN Shops with the smokestack visible while Jonathan Creek runs through this picture. Jones Lake is still decades away. The CN roundhouse was erected in the early 1922, part of a million dollar expansion that included diverting Jonathan Creek. The roundhouse allowed for the accommodation and repair of locomotives on tracks that radiated from a central turntable system to allow for maximum turning back and forth.

This big west end rail yard and roundhouse was south of Main Street near Chapman Street and included seven miles of track. The yard was demolished in

1961 to make way for the construction of the Hump Yard on the outskirts of the city. The old CN roundhouse was built to handle steam locomotives and while it could accommodate 40 railroad engines at a time, and featured an 85-foot turntable, the roundhouse was unable to be converted to handle the big diesel engines that CN introduced in the 1940s. Diesel engines were serviced at the repair shops off John Street and gradually as steam engines were replaced by diesel, the Newton Heights roundhouse became obsolete.

Barnes Circus Train Wreck, Canaan Station, July 20, 1930

A horrific train accident occurred north of Moncton at Canaan Station in 1930. It is since been known as the Barnes Circus Train Disaster. The Al. G. Barnes Circus was being hauled by a CN locomotive and had left Newcastle early one Sunday morning en route to Charlottetown. But at 7:00 A.M. while speeding south through Canaan Station, nine of the 29 cars were derailed in a pile-up that left a twisted mass of metal dispersed about the railway tracks. Four people died including three circus employees and a stowaway, later revealed to be James Stephen, a young man from outside Saint John. One of the victims, James Rogers of California, was rushed to the Moncton Hospital but died the same day while another seventeen passengers were also hospitalized for treatment and later released.

Fortunately, the animals, including twenty elephants and 300 horses, were housed in the front section of the rail car caravan and escaped unharmed since damages were confined to the back of the train. It had been a warm day and the

passengers who were riding outside in the open cars received the most damage
while most of the inside circus passengers escaped with only minor cuts and
bruises. However, the track was torn up for a considerable distance and train
traffic between Moncton and Rivière-du-Loup was suspended until repairs could
take place. An inquiry undertaken by a coroner's jury cited a falling arch bar to
be the most likely cause of the wreck. Eight witnesses gave evidence during the
hearing including the driver and conductor of the wreck. The jury ruled that an
overhanging object had most likely fallen onto the tracks and became wedged
under a passing circus car. The derailment and deaths were deemed accidental
and "no blame attached to anyone." The nine damaged cars were hauled into
the CN repair shops at Moncton and within a week, were repaired and ready to
continue touring the region. While the circus performers were recovering from
the mishap, they gave two unscheduled performances at the Speedway Grounds,
now the site of the D. N. D. grounds off Vaughan Harvey Boulevard. And the
Barnes Circus Train wreck remains to this day one of the biggest railway trag-
edies in Maritime Canada's railway history.

Humphrey Mill, CN and M&B Railway Tracks in Background, Moncton, 1931

John Humphrey had acquired an old water-powered mill on this site prior to
Confederation and after the Dominion National Policy was enacted to encourage
Canadian manufacturing, he established a woolen mill to serve the national

market. The fact that a railway ran through his backyard was also significant since Humphrey did not need to construct a spur line. He used the Intercolonial Railway to ship his famous Humphrey tweed pants and red & black checked mackinaws to markets throughout Canada and the United States. The company became known as John A. Humphrey & Son and by 1890, employed one hundred workers. The sprawling site included an industrial complex of seventeen rambling buildings that housed a dyehouse, sawmill, gristmill, horse barn, engine house, repair shop, smokestack, and various warehouses. John Humphrey died in 1895 and his son William F., successfully ran the business until 1934 when his son, William M. Humphrey, took over the operation. Humphrey's had record sales during both world wars supplying Canada's military but after World War II, the company ran into steep competition from central Canadian manufacturers.

The photo reveals the main building (still standing and modernized) on the left side of Mill Road while the warehouse building is standing on the right side of the road above the mill pond. The general office building is on the right below the pond, and both the warehouse and office building were demolished when a new bridge was erected in the 1970s. At the top of the picture, behind the woolen mill can be seen two CNR lines into Moncton and the Humphrey Railway Station (c1915) is on the right side of Mill Road.

One of the rail lines was the main CNR trunk line in and out of Moncton while the other track carried the Moncton and Bouctouche Railway that had been merged with CN in 1918. And between 1912 and 1917, Moncton's street cars also used these tracks to carry Monctonians out to Humphreys and back.

Spur Line, Reed Company Wharf, Moncton Waterfront, 1931

Moncton could once claim to have a working waterfront and this site at the foot of Mechanic Street was home to Joseph Salter's shipyard during the 1850s. This photo shows the Reed Company warehouses with two spur railway lines visible in the centre of the picture. The tracks ran along the waterfront from the main CN line upriver near the subway, eastward to the Public Wharf, and then across Main Street to Marven's Biscuit Factory. In the bottom right corner stands the city's first electric generating station.

The warehouses directly in back of the docked schooner were built after a fire had destroyed the first storage sheds in 1916. They were primarily used for the molasses trade since the Reed Company specialized in bringing in molasses by schooner and tramp steamer from Barbados, and other islands of the West Indies. The spur rail line had been developed in the 1880s to serve the old cotton mill and sugar refinery off Main Street and also served to connect with the Moncton and Bouctouche Railway that originally left Moncton by crossing Halls' Creek before heading north to Bouctouche. During this period, Eatons' mail order business was thriving, and became one of the largest users of CN's rail service throughout the Maritimes.

Women Working on a Freight Locomotive, c1944

During both World War I and II, the railway throughout Canada boomed as freight and troops were rushed to the east and west coasts to be shipped by convoy to the warfront. In 1941, Canadian Pacific alone moved 51 million tons of freight, double the total amount moved by rail in Canada in 1918. And especially during World War II, just as the need for workers mushroomed, thousands of railway workers left their jobs to join the armed forces. Over 40,000 men from the combined CNR and CPR railways joined the forces during the war and that left women to essentially provide the manpower to run Canada's two national railway systems. And women certainly rose to the occasion.

As well as serving directly in the armed forces both at home and abroad, women served as car cleaners, messengers, shop labourers, and stepped up to help with the on-going maintenance of the vast rolling stock and railway equipment needed to keep Canada's war effort alive. Some resistance from male quarters linger on but industry was simply desperate for workers and couldn't afford to maintain a "men only" policy in key industrial sectors. And the new federal government agency in charge of recruiting women into essential industries was also pushing hard to have women hired. On June 14, 1944, on orders from the Moncton office of the Selective Service Commission, Rita Leaman and Gladys Robinson became the first two women to be employed in the CNR railway shops.

Digging Out in a Miramichi Winter, c1900

Three miles south of Rogersville, stands Acadie Siding, situated along the main CN line, where trains head back and forth from Moncton and Montreal. But no traffic moved along the line on January 28, 1933 after a massive snowstorm rendered the area impassable with ten-foot drifts of packed snow. A snow plow special train left Moncton ahead of the northbound *Ocean Limited* but was stalled in a huge drift near Grangeville that even buried the engine's smoke stack. Meanwhile, an ill-fated southbound snow plow train had been dispatched from Newcastle under the competent charge of Moncton conductor F.J. Beers. Fred J. Beers had been born 47 years earlier in Kent County, was widely regarded by his railway associates and had been promoted to conductor during World War I. He also had a brother who worked as a brakeman for CN. Beers took charge of the snow plow train that January day and headed south to help clear the tracks. Two Moncton brakemen, H. Probert and J. MacCray were also on the special along with two Newcastle crewmen, Alex Astle and Martin English.

After reaching Rogersville around 6:00 pm, the storm began to gain in intensity but Beers plough on before becoming stalled in a deep drift at Acadie Siding. A furious blizzard soon made visibility impossible and a potentially deadly situation arose. The enormous all-weather, 16-wheel Northern locomotive No. 6116, the largest engine in the entire CNR system, was dispatched from Rogersville to clear the tracks. Veteran railway men claimed the big Northern could get through anything as long as there were still tracks underneath. Aboard the fired-up giant Northern, engineer Manning Renton and conductor N. Appleby knew there was a stalled train to the south but didn't have the exact location. At any rate, at 8:15 that evening, the Northern crashed practically through the entire snow van, wrecking it entirely, and killing instantly three railway men. The rear end collision ended the lives of Fred Beers, Alexander Astle, and Martin English, also injuring two snow shovelers from Newcastle, Fred Maltsis and Abel Boudreau. Two others on the snow plow, H. Probert and J. MacCray, were thrown from the train and escaped unharmed. Fortunately, no one was seriously hurt aboard the big steam locomotive.

When the news of the tragedy reached railway headquarters at Moncton, a relief train was dispatched to the dreadful scene of death, mangled steel, and iron. A large wrecking crane and clearing equipment came in from Campbellton. CN's General Manager, W. U. Appleton, was aboard the Moncton relief train as well as over fifty snow shovelers. Besides the collision at Acadie Siding, the main CN line was also blocked at Grangeville where a second snow plow remained stalled in snowdrifts. And sadly, aboard the stalled northbound train was brakeman W.W. Beers, brother of Fred Beers. The relief train arrived at Acadie Siding around midnight and it took all night for crews to clear the tracks. The south bound *Ocean Limited* was held at Rogersville until the following day while Montreal bound trains had not been allowed to exit Union Station at Moncton. The coroner was notified in Richibucto and Dr. T. J. Bourque allowed the bodies to be removed to Moncton and Newcastle where formal inquests were held. Both inquests came to the same conclusion that the accident was the unfortunate result of a blinding snowstorm, and little could have been done to prevent the accident except to cease all traffic along the CN in times of severe storms.

CN National Piggyback Service, c1958

This photo may have been taken at the Wallace Warehouse on Church Street in Moncton since the structure in the background resembles the old brick building that originally was erected in 1880 to house the Peter's Combination Lock Factory. The original railway piggyback system—horse and wagon riding on flatcars—was introduced in Canada in Nova Scotia in the 1850s but the innovation came from Britain where Scottish railway operator James Anderson had pioneered the idea. After World War II, railways were under seize by the trucking industry as significant freight contracts were being taken over by the highway truck system as a toll-free, national road system was developed throughout Canada. But in the 1950s, railways did a slight u-turn and embraced the trucking option.

In 1952, CN's arch rival, Canadian Pacific, became the first in North America to launch the intermodal rail system known as piggybacking, the precursor to containerization, whereby freight trailers were shipped long distances on flat railcars, and then transferred onto trailer trucks for local deliveries. The next year, CN adopted a similar service, initially inaugurated between Toronto and Montreal, and then nationally in the mid 1950s. CN promoted this service as the best of both worlds—local convenience and long-distance speed. CN even established a separate company called the National Rail Piggyback Service and within the Maritimes, the Speedway Express handled the regional freight service with its' head office located in Saint John. Major shareholders were Murray Macfie of St. Lambert, Quebec, Charles Palmer from Saint John, and Charles Parker of Hartland. New Brunswick Terminals were located in Saint John, Fredericton, Edmundston, Bathurst, and Moncton, while customers included many of the major local exporters such as Red Rose Tea, T.S. Simms, Crosby's Molasses, Conner's Bros, Thorne's Hardware Ltd, and Irving Oil.

CANADA EASTERN
RAILWAY

Railway Bridge at Blackville, c1895

This Ole Larsen photo shows tracks of the Canada Eastern Railway Company with the Southwest Miramichi River in the background. The Canada Eastern was built between South Devon opposite Fredericton to outside Chatham, a distance of almost 150 miles through some of the most difficult terrain in the province. The section of the line above Doaktown was built by Senator Jabez Snowball of Chatham while the southwest tracks from Doaktown to South Devon were erected by a partnership arrangement between Snowball and Alexander Gibson. The line opened for traffic in 1887 under the name Northern and Western Railway and two years later, the Fredericton Railway Bridge opened giving the railway direct access to downtown Fredericton. The Snowball-Gibson enterprise involved two powerful personalities working together, and when Senator Snowball voted to replace Boss Gibson as president, Gibson became so incensed that he refused to use his own railway to truck his cotton textiles to and from Fredericton. Every day for a year, horse and wagon shipments could be seen leaving the Marysville Cotton Mill and heading to Fredericton by road.

Eventually the partners settled their differences but fought often until Senator Snowball sold his shares in the railway to Gibson in 1893. For a short time, the railway and cotton mill were merged into a single company called the Alexander Gibson Railway and Manufacturing Company. But in the early 1900s, Boss Gibson's empire was on the ropes and the Intercolonial Railway took over the line in 1905 after the federal government purchased it for $819,000. In 1912, the Transcontinental Railway intersected the old Canada Eastern Railway at McGivney and for many decades, Frederictonians had excellent access to Upper Canada by taking the train to McGivney and jumping on to a NTR train that had become part of the CNR in the 1920s.

Old Woodburner, Indiantown, Canada Eastern Railway, c1887

Most early locomotives in New Brunswick were wood burning engines and a typical early locomotive burned a full cord of wood every 35 miles. Only a limited supply could be stocked on board so contracts with farmers and woodlot owners for delivery at "wooding-up" stations along the rail line was an important business transaction for the railway. As well, water for the steam boiler had to be available along the route, and many retired engineers could recall colourful stories of stopping at a stream to replenish their tank with brook water from a bucket. But the early trains also featured open smokestacks and boiler explosions from overheated engines often caused a number of accidents on board. Forest and barn fires from flying cinders were also common and would cause an outcry from nearby farmers and woodlot owners. After these early trains passed by, many a farmer could be seen rushing to rescue his cattle from a burning hay barn. Wire screen netting was installed over the smokestack to try and catch the burning cinders and a hopper was later added. Brakes were an afterthought on the first steam locomotives and one early American account claimed to have witnessed slave labourers attempting to slow an incoming train by inserting wooden stakes in the spokes. Hand brakes were later installed and brakemen had to be rugged individuals in order to slow or stop a train loaded with freight. Brake handles became known as "Armstrongs" and after individual freight cars became equipped with brakes, a "downbrake" whistle signal would result in a brakeman rushing along the top of a speeding car in search of the brake shank and wheel that was situated above the roof. Winter was especially hazardous since slippery conditions could mean falls and frozen equipment could cause brakes to fail to engage. The more efficient airbrakes remained rare in Maritime Canada until after 1900.

Steam Locomotive No. 21 at Blackville, c1900

This photo shows the railway crew along with a young girl and dog outside the Blackville Station on the Canada Eastern Railway line. The crew is blocking the wheel configuration but it is probably the common American wheel arrangement (4-4-0). The first steam locomotive in North America to burn coal and run over all-metal rails was the 15-metric ton *Samson* that transported coal for the Stellarton Albion Mines in Pictou County. Built in England, the *Samson* travelled ten kilometers per hour and in 1839, began hauling coal to waiting ships at Abercrombie. The ten-kilometer line had been constructed from locally produced iron rails. A Scottish engineer named Donald Thompson sat at the rear of the open locomotive, exposed to all kinds of weather. The Albion Mines railway was the second in Canada, and the earliest to use a standard gauge track and split-switch, movable rail. And in 1840, the Albion Mines railway became fully operational as a steam railway with three British built locomotives in service, *Samson, John Buddle*, and the *Hercules*. Prior to 1839, coal had been hauled along a tramway by horse-drawn rail cars.

This rail track was Canada's first and the cast-iron rails of this early line were also made at the Albion Mines. They are considered the first iron rails to be manufactured in North America. The *Samson* was used for about thirty years, then exhibited at the 1893 World's Fair in Chicago and returned to Pictou County in 1950. Containing almost all its original parts, the *Samson* is North America's oldest surviving steam locomotive and the second oldest existing British Hackworth engine. New Brunswick's first locomotive, *Hercules*, was purchased in Boston and arrived by boat at Shediac in 1854 while a second locomotive, also called *Samson*, was unloaded at Moncton around the same time. Another US built locomotive, the *St. John*, out of Portland, Maine, was the first locomotive to haul along the pioneer European & North American Railway between Saint John and Rothesay.

Early engine drivers were rough and ready men, many had been hired out of Scotland, and besides having to be a jack-of-all-trades, a pioneer engineer drove his engines on an open deck, fully exposed to the elements. An engineer arriving at a train station with a dirty face from flying cinders was a common sight at many Maritime railway stations before Confederation. Another fascinating subject for railway historians is railway gauge since the standard gauge of 4' 8-1/2" between parallel rails was not always standard. A number of different gauge sizes were established including the British broad gauge (5' 6") that was initially adopted by the Intercolonial Railway, and the narrow 3' 6" gauge of Boss Gibson's New Brunswick Railway. During the Civil War era, American federal forces were threatening to invade Canada and adopting the British broad gauge was actually viewed as a security measure since it promised to prevent American trains from entering Canada.

Main Street, Boiestown, Railway Station on Left, c1905

Boiestown is located about halfway between Fredericton and Newcastle. The community was established as a sawmill company town in the early 1800s by Thomas Boies and remained essentially a lumber town during the 1800s. Situated on the Southwest Miramichi River, salmon fishing became an important past time in the late 1800s as anglers from all over North America were drawn to the fishing lodges and camps along the river. These tourist-anglers came into Boiestown by rail and directly across the street from the train station stands the Duffy Hotel where sportsmen could stay until departing for the wilderness camps. The Duffy Hotel was operated by the Duffy family and competed for lodgers with the nearby Traveller's Inn, out of sight on the left, behind the station. On the right, behind the Duffy Hotel is situated the Campbell house that is still standing today.

Lumber Mill at Chatham, ICR in Foreground, c1900

Jabez Snowball was the leading industrialist in Chatham during the late 1800s and built a 9-mile rail line called the Chatham Branch Railway in the 1870s to connect with the ICR. In the 1880s, Senator Snowball, along with Boss Gibson, constructed the Canada Eastern Railway west from Chatham to Fredericton. Eventually, the ICR took the line over but Snowball also had opened the largest steam sawmill in New Brunswick during the 1870s. He became the second largest provincial lumber exporter during the 1880s, employing over 1000 men. During his best years, Jabez Snowball's mill operations ended up milling over 170,000 board feet of lumber per day. He also established the Miramichi Steam Navigation Company and the Chatham Telephone Exchange. Snowball also served in both the House of Commons and the Canada Senate. In 1902, he was appointed New Brunswick's Lieutenant Governor. He died in 1907 at the age of 69 and while he died a wealthy man with many on-going business interests including Chatham's largest lumber mill, his businesses were not maintained by his family and the mill closed in 1919.

Posing for Camera, Chatham Railway Station, c1890

This solid little station is still standing today and was erected in the 1870s to serve the tiny 9-mile Chatham Branch Railway that had been constructed by Senator Jabez Snowball to connect with the Intercolonial Railway. The railway had been completed exactly one month after the ICR had opened on July 1, 1876. A decade later, the Chatham Branch line became the eastern end of the Canada Eastern Railway that was built from the ICR to Fredericton. The line was later extended five miles east to Loggieville but the Chatham station remained the major station for the Canada Eastern Railway since the town served as the distribution centre for the Miramichi River Valley. Today, a number of other interesting old railway stations in New Brunswick remain standing including at Minto, St. Andrews, Rogersville, Kedgewick, St. Stephen, Rothesay, and even at Campbellton where a modern tourist information centre has been erected based on the architecture of the old station. Of the hundreds of old railway stations constructed throughout the Maritimes, about seventy are still standing and while a number have been converted into museums and heritage centres, they still are disappearing at an alarming rate.

Railway Crew at Chatham Station, c1900

The Canada Eastern Railway opened in 1887 and few people remember that for a time, this line had a daily train named after a ghost. Most New Brunswickers vaguely know about the Dungarvon Whooper legend and many versions are still told around campfires each summer. The legend has also been weaved into a song by the famous Miramichi poet, Michael Whelan. Each verse of Whelan's song ends with the line "Where the dark and deep Dungarvon rolls along" and recounts the story of a tragic death in a lumber camp deep inside the Renous woods.

The Dungarvon woods stretch along the river of the same name in central New Brunswick above Quarryville. Around the time of Confederation, an Irishman named Ryan wandered into a Dungarvon lumber camp. The camp needed a cook and the cheerful young man was hired. He seemed a perfect fit since he obviously knew how to cook for a large crew, and could yell and holler better than anyone—a great quality for waking up a lumber camp before dawn. Popular among the crew, the youthful cook carried a large money belt around his waist and it became common knowledge that the belt contained a large amount of cash. One day, the new boss stayed in camp with the cook while everyone else left for the woods.

What happened that autumn day is anyone's guess but when the men returned to camp that evening, Ryan the cook was dead and his money belt had disappeared. The boss was a big man in an age when might was right, and no one challenged him when he declared that the cook had died of a sudden illness despite the fact he seemed quite healthy at breakfast that morning. A gathering snowstorm turned into a blinding blizzard but the men were determined to give Ryan a proper burial. They dug a grave and buried him beside the nearby Dungarvon spring. That night, back at the lumber camp, a chilling cry was heard in the direction of the spring, and the whooping sounds began to echo throughout the forest. The unearthly screams resembled the great hollers that Ryan the cook would undertake each morning and the lumber crew were convinced that the screams were originating at the spring gravesite. After a few evening of uninterrupted whooping, the crew left the haunted Dungarvon woods never to return. Thus forth, reports of a whooping ghost at work each night in the Dungarvon woods were common.

Folks along the Southwest Miramichi became so enraged with this superstition that they sought help from the Miramichi's religious establishment. Many strange tales were told including claims that the gravesite would not freeze up in winter, flowers bloomed all year at the site, frying bacon would often attract the ghost, and shrieking screams could sometimes follow a woodsmen. Rev. Edward Murdock, parish priest of Renous was sought out to try and exorcised the evil spirit and became convinced that the mysterious Dungarvon Whooper was indeed the ghost of the murdered cook. He traveled to Dungarvon and read the church service of exorcism. Reports of a decrease in ghostly activity were noted after Rev. Murdock's visit but then, the famous Miramichi wit became involved when the railway was constructed between Fredericton and the Miramichi. The daily train on the Canada Eastern Railway Company line was nicknamed the "Whooper" since it traveled near the Dungarvon woods.

Noted Miramichi historian, Louise Manny, told the following story of the Whooper train: "The first train that ran from Quarryville to Newcastle was loaded with Dungarvon River Lumberjacks celebrating their weekend off with riotous hilarity that is characteristic of high-spirited men suddenly freed from monotonous isolation. They shouted, they sang, they told raucous jokes, they drank, not necessarily in that order. Every time the train blew its whistle, they whooped up an ear-splitting echoing chorus. When innocently asked what train this was, with a sigh, the patient conductor answered 'The Dungarvon Whooper.' So that was what it was called throughout the four decades the railway service was operated, until 1936. It was the first train in the world named in honour of a ghost."

Train Pulling Into Taymouth Station, c1901

Taymouth Station served the Canada Eastern Railway between Fredericton and Chatham that ran up along the Nashwaak Valley before heading over the high country to Boiestown and the Miramichi. Along the Nashwaak Valley, railway bridges were constructed across the river at Sandyville above Marysville, at Penniac, and above Taymouth at Nashwaak Bridge. These three bridges were all built of wood when they opened in 1887 but after the Intercolonial Railway took over the Canada Eastern they rebuilt the bridges with steel. But the line still suffered from loose ballast and unstable sleepers that prevented the line from using the new heavy locomotives that could haul larger trains.

Eventually, the ICR and then the CNR upgraded the entire line laying new underpinnings and ballast but the line still suffered from the rough terrain that characterized central New Brunswick. Delays were frequent especially crossing over the Sandyville Bridge and another frustration for passengers occurred after the York and Carleton Railway branch line was built from Cross Creek Crossing to Stanley. Passengers between Fredericton and the Miramichi would suffer the daily inconvenience of having to wait at Cross Creek Station on a spur line until the Stanley passengers arrived.

Fredericton Intercolonial Railway Station, c1903

Fredericton's second railway station came about as the result of the railway bridge being completed across the St. John River in 1888. Both the New Brunswick Railway (to Edmundston) and the Canada Eastern Railway (from Chatham) had been largely built through the efforts of Boss Gibson and had ended at Gibson (South Devon) on the north side of the river. Once the bridge allowed traffic to be extended into the city, headquarters for the Canada Eastern Railway were moved to a site on the south side of Brunswick Street where a station was quickly erected. The Canada Eastern line now offered passenger and freight service across the river to connect with the Intercolonial Railway. Frederictonians then had a choice in railway travel—east to the ICR or west on the CPR.

After Boss Gibson became over extended financially in the early 1900s, the Canada Eastern Railway (also called for a period the Northern and Western Railway) was purchased by the federal government for $819,000 and handed over to the ICR to operate. This station and the line east to the Miramichi became part of the ICR rail network. In 1911, the structure was demolished in favour of a new station that became Fredericton's ICR headquarters. In the 1920s, the ICR was folded into the Canadian National Railway system and this station became the Fredericton CNR Station. It too was demolished in the 1960s.

South Devon Railway Station, c1920

The first railway station on the north side of the St. John River across from Fredericton was erected in the early 1870s at South Devon (then called Gibson) to serve as the southern terminus for the New Brunswick Railway that had been built by Alexander Gibson. Gibson needed a railway to help develop huge timber stands north of Fredericton but he also wanted to exploit timber lands east towards the Miramichi and became involved in constructing the Canada Eastern Railway to Chatham. Once the railway bridge was constructed across the St. John River to Fredericton, a new north-side station was needed and this second South Devon station was erected on the south side of Union Street near the entrance to the railway bridge.

Ted and Anita Jones, in their book *Historic Fredericton North*, note that this station was actually constructed after the ICR took over the Canada Eastern Railway in 1904. The station remained in use by the ICR, and then the CNR, until 1937 when a new railway bridge across the St. John was built to replace the old railway bridge destroyed in the great 1936 flood. Once the new bridge was built, a new station further back from the bridge was built near Barker Street.

South Devon CN Roundhouse, c1940

This Walter Long photograph shows the new roundhouse and engine room built in 1937 in South Devon west of Barker Street after the second railway bridge was erected across the St. John River. The engine house featured seven engine stalls and the turntable can be seen in the front of the building. The turntable facility allowed for the repair of locomotives on tracks that could be rotated for turning expediency. Canadian National's central New Brunswick headquarters for repairs took place in South Devon, as well as in nearby McGivney Station where CN's main trunk line ran from Moncton to Edmundston. Fredericton had tried without success to be on a major transcontinental corridor whereby the CPR would have built their major trunk line from Harvey Station through the city. The route would have then run across the railway bridge to Salisbury and on to Halifax where running rights over the Intercolonial Railway tracks would have been acquired. City fathers were anxious for this to occur and even moved their race track in 1886 in anticipation of the line coming through. Yet this so called "Short Line" to Montreal was indeed built by the CPR in 1889 but bypassed the capital city in favour of the port of Saint John.

Suburban Train, Marysville Station, 1905

In 1886, industrialist Alexander Gibson opened the largest cotton mill in Canada at Marysville employing 500 workers the first year. The number of employees would almost double in the 1890s and after the Fredericton Railway Bridge opened, it became possible to have workers commute by rail back and forth from Fredericton to Marysville. Gibson's Canada Eastern Railway ran daily trains from Fredericton to Chatham and so in 1893, the Canada Eastern launched a new short train service called the *Suburban*. The shuttle train operate six round trips a day between the city and the Marysville Station opposite the cotton mill. Within a month of launching the service, it proved so popular that a seventh round trip was added. A round trip cost twenty cents and twenty-five one-way trips cost $1.40. Service began out of Fredericton at 6:15 am while the last train out of Marysville was at 9:20 pm. Gibson sold the Canada Eastern Railway in 1904 to the federal government but their Intercolonial Railway maintained the Suburban service until 1933.

Marysville Cotton Mill and Railway Line, c1903

This postcard shows the Gibson cotton mill on the upper right with the worker's residence in the background. In the foreground is the Canada Eastern Railway line that brought workers into the mill from Fredericton and shipped textiles to markets all over North America. Behind the smoke stack of the lumber mill can be seen the bridge across the Nashwaak River that connected the mill with the railway line. Alexander Gibson first began sawmill operations at Lepreau in Charlotte County, and then moved to York County where he purchased a number of Nashwaak Valley lumber mills. He then began buying up huge tracts of New Brunswick's timberlands. Initially concentrating on lumber, Gibson's timber tracts became massive and at one point, included half the forests of York County. He also began building other sawmills, including one at Blackville on the Miramichi.

With no rail connections above Fredericton, Gibson began in 1870 to build a narrow gauge railway through his timber lands to Edmundston. Later, in partnership with Senator J.B. Snowball, he built a railway from Fredericton to connect with the Intercolonial Railway at Chatham. In 1877, he helped build the first railway bridge across the St. John River at Fredericton but with Macdonald's National Policy promoting Canadian manufacturing in place, Boss Gibson turned to the production of cotton and erected one of Canada's largest cotton mills at Marysville. The main structure is still standing today. When complete, the company town of Marysville resembled a feudal village. As the province's largest timber baron and a big employer, Alexander Gibson maintained a firm grip on his industrial empire until about 1900 when it began to crumble due to brutal outside competition, high debt, and poor commercial prospects. The cotton mill was sold to Montreal interests in 1908, and the grand old man of the Nashwaak died at age 94 in 1913.

FREDERICTON
BRANCH RAILWAY

Engine No. 2, York Street Crossing, Fredericton, c1874

This George Taylor photograph shows Alexander Gibson (white beard) and Fred Edgecombe standing on the right. Gibson was the leading industrialist and railway man in Fredericton at the time, and Fred Edgecombe was the Fredericton Branch Railway's first ticket agent. Edgecombe became superintendent in 1875 and along with partner E.R. Burpee, leased the line from the Fredericton Branch Railway Company the same year, operating the railway between the city and Fredericton Junction until it became absorbed into the New Brunswick Railway. In the background stands the Exhibition Palace, built in 1864 and then destroyed by fire in 1877. The No.2 locomotive was built in New Jersey and equipped in Fredericton with an adjustable railway flanger that is visible at the bottom of the front of the engine. This railway innovation was invented by Black Frederictonian railwayman John Hamilton. Hamilton worked at the

Devon roundhouse for Gibson's New Brunswick Railway, and was described as a strong, versatile employee, able to perform all railway tasks, including building and maintaining equipment. The railway flanger was used for debris and snow removal, consisting of a pair of iron blades attached to the locomotive pilot that rode close to the rails and could be raised or lowered by a lever in the cab. The device was adopted as standard equipment by the Fredericton Railway Company but began causing problems once stop signs were installed. This kind of flanger was eventually abandoned but not before it was patented. Records show, however, that the Hamilton flanger was actually patented as the Miller flanger, named for the railway's branch engineer, Henry Miller. It's not known whether Hamilton sold his invention to Miller.

Victoria Mill, Railway Tracks in Foreground, Lower Fredericton, c1895

This photograph shows the Victoria Lumber Mill on the Lincoln Road, where today a marine is located. In the 1840s, steam engines made lumber mills quite profitable in New Brunswick and Captain Robert Chestnut built the Victoria Steam Saw and Manufacturing Establishment at the cove below the town. While the mill changed ownership a number of times, it developed into a large mill by Confederation with two gangs of saws including edging and trimming circulars and lath machinery. Once the Fredericton Branch Railway erected tracks to connect with the Western Extension Railway at Fredericton Junction and on to Bangor, the mill began exporting large amounts of sawed lumber to the United States. It burned in 1892 but was immediately rebuilt. Owned by Hale & Muchie in the late 1800s, the Victoria Mill became the largest sawmill in Fredericton and in 1895, it processed over ten million feet of logs. Just prior to World War I, the mill was acquired by the Fraser Company and in addition to producing saw lumber, began producing large quantities of wooden shingles.

Fredericton Union Railway Station, c1935

Mayor W.G. Clark, front row left and Premier A.A. Dysart, third from left, with visiting business dignitaries, including CPR president Edward Beatty, second from left. This brick station was erected in 1923 after Fredericton's first wooden train station, built in 1869, was deemed obsolete. The Fredericton Branch Railway was built by the Fredericton Railway Company to connect the 22 miles from the capital city to Hartts Mills (Fredericton Junction). It opened for traffic in 1869 and linked Fredericton with the Western Extension Railway from Saint John to Bangor. This link and the entire Western extension was eventually taken over by the CPR but by the time this photo was taken in the 1930s, both the CPR and the CNR were using this station and hence the name union.

When the first station opened on York Street in 1869, two trains a day ran to Saint John but the location was considered out of the way by Frederictonians and attempts were undertaken to have the line extended from Salamanca along the river to the downtown Phoenix Square. A new railway station would have been constructed but railway officials and city politicians could not agree on this extension. In the end, the federal government had other plans for their military property near Phoenix Square and so the York Street station remained the city's railway station for all CPR traffic in and out of the city. During the early 1900s, CPR competed with the ICR-CNR railway that was headquartered on Brunswick Street. But Fredericton would not remain a two-railway station city. In the 1930s, with railway traffic deeply affected by the Depression, all railway passenger traffic was consolidated at this station.

Honeymoon Couple, Mr. & Mrs. Arthur Alexander, Fredericton Junction, 1915

Hartts Mills (Fredericton Junction) is situated 22 miles southwest of Fredericton. In the 1860s, the people of New Brunswick were clamoring for railways and the Legislature enacted the Railways Facility Act in 1864 promising a subsidy of $10,000 for every mile of railway construction that was completed in the colony. One of the most important lines to receive attention was the so-called Western Extension (of the European & North American Railway) to connect New Brunswick with the railways throughout the United States. Maine promised to build from Bangor to the New Brunswick border and so the Western Extension Railway would be built from West Saint John to the Maine border.

The only question was where would it cross the border, the most direct route to Bangor via Stephen-Calais, or further north? St. Stephen and the people of Charlotte County had high hopes for the Western extension to come through their community but the politicians in Fredericton had control over the construction subsidy. Consequently, the line was built north to allow a rail connection with the provincial capital. And so Hartts Mills became Fredericton Junction as the Fredericton Branch Railway was built the 22 miles from the capital city. The branch opened in 1869 and allowed the citizens of Fredericton to travel by rail to meet the Western Extension Railway from Saint John and travel on to McAdam, Bangor, Boston or Montreal.

American Sportsmen, Fredericton Junction, 1944

New Brunswick was considered a paradise for hunting and fishing by Americans in the early 1900s after much of the American wilderness had been fished and hunted to extinction. British officers were first to sing the praises of New Brunswick in the 1800s but soon American sportsmen were traveling by steamer to fish the major salmon rivers of the Restigouche, Miramichi, Nepisiguit, and the St. John. Once railways were built and reliable connections were established with the major American cities, the popularity of salmon angling and sport adventures in the wilds of New Brunswick took off.

The coming of the Yankee fishermen in pursuit of big fish and game began in earnest with the writings of Charles Lanman, who wrote a popular and comical adventure story chronicling his backwoods experiences. *Adventures of an Angler in Canada, Nova Scotia, and the United States* was published in 1848. Charles Lanman knew salmon fishing, and became acquainted with many of the best angling sites including the Nepisiguit River where near Grand Falls he claimed the first salmon in New Brunswick were caught with a fly rod and artificial fly. This bountiful site became his favourite and he often praised it, "No more than half a dozen persons have yet done much in the way of angling at the Grand Falls, and the most successful and persevering one of all, by far, comes all the way from England to throw the fly at this very spot, and during the season of 1850 captured no less than three hundred and twenty salmon and grilse within the space of two months."

Lady Macdonald laying the cornerstone of the first railway bridge, Fredericton, August 15, 1887

This photograph shows Lady Macdonald placing a tin box with issues of local newspapers and coins into the cornerstone on the riverbank at the head of Waterloo Row. Numerous dignitaries at the historic ceremony included Sir John A. Macdonald seated with a cane in the upper right corner above the excavation. Lieutenant-Governor Samuel Leonard Tilley is standing to the left of Lady Macdonald and Senator Thomas Temple is on the right of Lady Macdonald. Senator Temple operated a river steamboat and served as president of the Fredericton Railway Company. He was also managing director of the Fredericton and St. Mary's Railway Bridge Company with the responsibility to build the huge structure across the St. John River.

Alexander Gibson was president of the bridge company and while the bridge was indeed a local enterprise with Temple and Gibson as investors, plus F.R. Burpee and F.S. Hilyard, the Dominion government under Sir John A. Macdonald had done the actual incorporation, provided much of the working capital, and had final jurisdiction over all construction projects over Canadian navigational waters. A railway bridge over the St. John River had been discussed for fifteen years and at one point in the early 1880s, a combination road and railway bridge had been proposed by Premier Andrew Blair. However, in 1885, a sole highway bridge was built. Macdonald's Dominion government were champions of the railway bridge and introduced a bill in Parliament to construct a short line railway from Upper Canada that would pass through Fredericton and over the

Saint John River to Salisbury connecting with the ICR. Yet the bill was defeated in the Senate and an actual short line was built but not through Fredericton. But the Fredericton and St. Mary's Railway Bridge went ahead and on June 15, 1888, the first engine crossed the river and five days later, the first two passenger cars filled to capacity went back and forth

First Crossing, Fredericton Railway Bridge, June 15, 1888

The photo shows the first locomotive to cross the bridge from Fredericton to Devon hauling four flat cars including the last car full of workmen that had help build the bridge. Gilmore Brown designed the bridge while the Dominion Bridge Company Ltd. of Lachine, Quebec, built the structure that took over 12 months to complete. The Fredericton Railway Bridge was the largest bridge to be built in New Brunswick when it was complete in 1888, and featured nine spans with granite piers. The granite had been hauled in from Spoon Island and the fill was freestone that had been quarried in New Maryland as well as in Nelson Hollow on the Miramichi. Work had continued throughout the winter of 1887-88, and a first for the area was the use of electric lights to aid construction.

The bridge featured a level crossing at both ends and provided an interconnection with all the rail lines in and around Fredericton. And while the bridge did not end up serving a trunk line, it did accommodate the Canada Eastern Railway, the New Brunswick Railway, and the Fredericton Branch Railway, moving freight and passengers back and forth to Edmundston, Maine, and the Miramichi. Eventually, in the 1920s, the bridge was shared by both national railways, the CNR and the CPR, and became the major St. John River crossing point for trains running east and west.

Fredericton Railway Bridge With Draw Span Open, c1900

The Dominion government had been a major financial partner in the construction of the Fredericton Railway Bridge that opened in 1888 and the federal authorities were also responsible for all navigational waters in Canada including rivers. The St. John River winds through two countries, and even today, has substantial river traffic. One federal condition considered mandatory before commencing construction was that the bridge would include a draw section allowing large riverboats to continue to travel upriver.

This photo shows the draw out allowing passage up and down the river. While the Fredericton Railway Bridge was a grand accomplishment and served central New Brunswick well for many years, it did not make money. The Fredericton and St. Mary's Railway Bridge Company had built the structure but the federal government essentially held the mortgage and expected that bridge tolls would eventually pay the freight. But the bridge never hosted a main national line, and the local traffic was not enough to even pay the interest on the debt. Industrial Alexander Gibson had been president and a major investor in the bridge company and when his fortunes declined rapidly in the early 1900s, the Dominion government pulled the plug on the venture and foreclosed in 1904. Despite a year's reprieve, the situation did not improve and in 1905, the bridge became part of the federal Intercolonial Railway system since Gibson's Eastern Railway between Chatham and Fredericton had also been taken over by the ICR.

Destruction of the Railway Bridge, Fredericton, March 19, 1936

This photograph shows Waterloo Row after the big March break-up. On the left is a piece of the railway bridge that had been torn off the piers. Most of the steel structure was resting at the bottom of the river but this piece was swept up on the riverbank by the huge ice flows. According to Ted Jones in his book *Fredericton Flashback*, the March 19th break-up on the St. John River was the earliest breakdown of the ice at Fredericton since records first began to be recorded in 1825. It was also one of the largest floods in recorded history.

First Passenger Train Crossing the Second Fredericton Railway Bridge, June 1, 1938

Fredericton's first highway bridge to the north side had been completed in 1885 and was called "Blair's paper bridge" in honour of Premier Andrew Blair since critics predicted that a bridge across the St. John would not hold during the freshet season. However, they were wrong, and the bridge remained in place despite major floods for 20 years until fire destroyed the structure. However, the railway bridge was another matter. The first Fredericton Railway Bridge had been built with level crossings at each end and so the bridge's height was essentially the same as the two banks of the river. And as the swelling river overflowed its banks each spring, the danger of damage to the structure became a concern. March and April freshets were yearly occurrences, but some years the floods of water and ice were severe and would rise over the bridge. One of the worst years was 1936 and on March 19, the river took the bridge away, making over half a mile of steel vanish to the bottom of the river.

Hundreds of Frederictonians along Waterloo Road witnessed the destruction as the river reached 30 feet, and flooding occurred throughout the downtown. Huge mounds of river ice were everywhere and the bridge steel spans were simply lifted off the granite piers and swept away. Once the flooding receded, it was determined that a new railway bridge would be built at the same location but would be an additional six feet in height in order to prevent further destruction from floods. Work began the same year, and subways at both ends of the bridge allowed trains to proceed off the bridge and overtop Waterloo Row and Union Street in South Devon. The official opening of the second bridge was June 1, 1938 and today, the old bridge is still standing, serving the community as a walking trail across the river.

Return of the Carleton-York Regiment, Fredericton Railway Station, 1945

Railways were developed to move people and freight, and war brought this movement into high gear. Both World War I & II placed huge demands on Canada's transcontinental railway system. Numerous troop and cargo trains transported men and goods to the east coast ports of Saint John and Halifax where ships waited to sail to overseas destinations. On the busiest day during World War I, 38 trains brought 14,000 troops to Halifax via the Intercolonial Railway and Moncton, as the ICR and NTR headquarters, became famous for its speedy repair service and great hospitality.

Volunteer brass bands welcome the troop trains, designated as "specials" in railroad lingo, and one day during the war, eleven specials were greeted in Moncton by booming music. By 1915, the inevitable hospital trains began to haul the wounded back to waiting Canadian hospitals, and the dark green cars with Military Hospital stamped across side were given priority over all other traffic along the ICR line. Hospital cars were constructed at the Moncton shops and other special WWI trains included the secret "silk" and "fish" trains. Unknown to the Canadian public, silk trains no longer carried delicate silk cocoons but instead, Chinese migrants from British Columbia were delivered to Halifax where they were sent overseas to assist in the Allied war effort. Fish trains were the code name for incoming gold shipments to Canada from Allied countries that help pay for the war supplies. In all, over a billion dollars in gold bullion passed through the New Brunswick ICR line all under the watchful eyes of heavily armed guards.

CANADIAN
PACIFIC

New Brunswick Railway Station, McAdam Junction, c1887

McAdam was a logging site known as Camp City when New Brunswick's first railway, the St. Andrews and Quebec Railway, went through in 1858. As a railway watering station, it was renamed McAdam Junction in honour of Charlotte County politician and lumberman John McAdam (1807-1893), and then shortened to McAdam in 1941. As the New Brunswick Railway began consolidating a number of branch lines in western New Brunswick in the 1880s, the "junction" near the Maine border became the major divisional hub for traffic heading west to Maine. The junction also could route traffic north to Edmundston, east to Fredericton, or south to St. Stephen or Saint John. In 1884, the New Brunswick Railway had become a far-flung line and consolidated their service and repair shops at McAdam Junction, closing out their facilities in St. Andrews. Forty-seven employees worked there and over sixteen trains went through the junction each day. When Canadian Pacific officially took over the New Brunswick Railway in 1890, McAdam took off with 125 people working there in the early 1890s, expanding to several hundred during World War I. McAdam was an entry point for the CPR's popular "Short Line" from Saint John through Maine to Montreal. Throughout the early years of the 1900s, the community was similar to Moncton—one of the Maritimes' busiest railway centres. This bustling station also doubled as a CP hotel but in the 1890s was deemed too small to adequately serve the booming traffic.

CPR Station, McAdam Junction, c1895

McAdam's first railway station is shown in the foreground in this classic railway photograph revealing the rail yard that was beginning to sprawl with activity, buildings, and equipment. This photo was taken just prior to Canadian Pacific's decision to build an elaborate new railway station. As the major railway crossroad in western New Brunswick, McAdam Junction was fondly remembered by travellers coming in to the province for visits and summer vacations. Willa Walker in her splendid book on St. Andrews, *No Hay Fever and a Railway*, vividly recalls family trips as a child travelling to St. Andrews from Montreal. Walker remembered the thrill of leaving Montreal in late June for an overnight trip on a Pullman, breakfast in the dinning car, her parents dealing with immigration inspectors at the border in Vanceboro, and then the most exciting time—arrival at McAdam Junction. "You could smell the different air. It was New Brunswick, of course!"

Walker also recalled that Montreal passengers going on to St. Andrews were required to wait at the station for the Boston train before the daily St. Andrews train could be dispatched. And in the early 1900s, a Miss Flora Grant ran the McAdam station and restaurant with such respect and decorum that it was considered proper manners for all CP employees from the very top on down, to pay their respects to Miss Grant when passing through McAdam.

CPR Station at McAdam Junction, c1904

McAdam's second railway station was built in 1900 to accommodate the expanding railway business that had occurred in 1889 after the CPR took over the majority of railway lines in western New Brunswick. This structure measured 133 feet x 36 feet, and was designed for the CPR by Edward Maxwell. The steeply-pitched roof and dormer windows characterized the Chateau Style of architecture favoured by the CPR in this period and its walls of local granite give the station a distinctive appearance. The basement included the boiler room and coal pile, kitchen and laundry room, while the first floor featured a general waiting room, a ladies' waiting room, ticket room, baggage and freight rooms, toilets, lunch counter, and dining room. The third floor contained railway offices, freight and custom offices, hotel bedrooms, a reading room as well as a bathroom while the top floor had four bedrooms reserved for hotel staff.

In 1911, two wings were added by CPR architect Walter Painter with the west wing containing an expanded dinning room plus additional hotel rooms and staff space. The east wing contained large baggage and express rooms. The CPR Station at McAdam was one of the largest and most ambitious railway stations built by the CPR in eastern Canada. While the hotel was closed out in 1959, the station remained a vibrant rail structure until the line through McAdam was closed out in the late 1990s. The old station is still standing and has been declared a National Historic Site.

Canadian Pacific Hotel, McAdam, c1905

McAdam's first railway station also lodged railway guests when the station was part of the New Brunswick Railway. But it became inadequate once the CPR acquired the line and expanded the service in the 1890s. CP built a bustling new station in 1900 and also constructed this hotel near the station. Railway business through McAdam Junction was brisk due in part to a virtual monopoly on passenger and freight traffic to and from the United States. As well the CPR's "Short Line" cut many hours off a Montreal to Saint John trip when compared to a Moncton to Montreal train trip via the ICR line along the remote north shore, and the St. Lawrence River. And until the National Transcontinental Railway opened in 1912, most of the upper St. John River Valley traffic was diverted south to McAdam before steaming northwest to Montreal. Indeed by 1910, with Saint John as Canada's Winter Port, McAdam Junction was the CPR's busiest railway station east of Montreal and handled dozens of CP train daily and hundreds of passengers. Only Moncton, as the ICR headquarters and repair centre, could rival the little railway junction for railway traffic in New Brunswick.

McAdam, City Camp Hotel on Far Left, c1930

McAdam was a roaring railway centre when this photograph was taken and the reason why this little out-of-the way lumber camp became a railway town is interesting.

The great feat of the Canadian Pacific Railway was reaching the Pacific Ocean from eastern Canada in 1885 after suffering financial hardships, rebellions, and a series of natural disasters. British Columbia had entered Confederation in 1871 and had been promised a railway to the Pacific. The last pike ceremony on November 7, 1885 saw CP financier Donald Smith finally drive in the final spike to complete the railway. And this historic feat is seen by Canadians almost everywhere as the true beginnings of nationhood. Now a transcontinental railway stretched across the vast northwest interior of North America. And CP officials then saw the opportunity to haul vast amounts of lucrative prairie grain back to Montreal to ship to markets across the world. Yet one problem remained. For four months each year, the St. Lawrence River was frozen solid and ships were unable to make the voyage up and down the river. Numerous historians had offered conjectures about why Canadian Pacific turned east, and built a rail line to the east coast.

One theory includes the notion that President Sir William Van Horne was quite fond of the area around St. Andrews and wanted a personal rail link from Montreal to his vacation home. Yet the fact remains that CP would have been unable to earn a significant amount of revenue four months out of every year without an ice-free port on the east coast. Once CP became an exporter of western wheat, they needed to ship year-round, and Saint John was the nearest ice-free port from Montreal. And the shortest distance from Montreal was through Maine to McAdam where the Western Extension Railway already linked the border town with Saint John. Consequently McAdam's prosperity can be said to have been the direct result of Canadian snow and ice.

Vanceboro Railway Station, Maine, c1883

The European and North American between Saint John and Shediac had been completed in 1860 and immediately the benefits of a railway westward to Maine became obvious. The Maine Central between Bangor and Portland and the Grand Truck Railway between Portland and Montreal had been built, and the missing link for full connections to the fast-growing United States and the Canadas was a line from Bangor to the border and on to Saint John. It would take almost a decade but the 88-mile Western Extension Railway from Carleton on the west side of Saint John to McAdam Junction opened in 1869.

Built by E.R. Burpee with significant financial support from industrialist William Parks, as well as the province and the city of Saint John, the line began at Fairville, and ran up along the St. John River to Welsford. It then wandered along the South Oromocto River where at Hartts Mill it met up with the Fredericton Branch Railway before heading west to Harvey Station and McAdam. The American portion of the Western Extension Railway of the European and North American from the border at Vanceboro to Bangor took a few years longer to build. The city of Bangor became the driving force for the line during the mid 1860s by providing financial aid and the State of Maine provided a series of land grants. By 1869, the railroad had been extended from Bangor through Milford to Mattawamkeag. Two years later, the Maine section of the Western Extension Railway had been completed to Vanceboro with a bridge connection over the St. Croix River and Maine-New Brunswick border to McAdam. On October 19, 1871, a grand last-spike ceremony was undertaken at Vanceboro with US President Ulysses S. Grant and Dominion Governor-General Lord Lisgar in attendance. Despite the fact the Western Extension Railway had been built in the British broad gauge and the Maine Central used standard gauge tracks, thereby causing serious delays in transporting railway cars through the entire line to Montreal or Boston, the grand dream of a western railway connecting New Brunswick with the US and Upper Canada had been completed.

Grain Fire, West Saint John, c1931

Western grain had been a valuable export commodity for Saint John beginning in the 1890s with Canadian Pacific establishing a grain elevator on the west side and working with the Beaver Line to establish Saint John as Canada's Winter Port. But fire was a constant worry since grain in storage would become dry and dusty. The port city's worst grain fire occurred on June 22, 1931 when a small fire broke out in a bathroom at Shed 7 on the west side. A United Fruit Company steamer had been unloading fruit and packing straw quickly caught fire engulfing the entire pier, spreading to other facilities including the nearby concrete grain terminal. Despite fire trucks reaching the site within minutes, the massive fire overwhelmed fire fighters and they were forced to abandon one pumper.

The UFC steamer *Gundersen* was moved to safety out into the harbour but the pilot vessel *Glooscap* and one CP steamer caught fire and both were destroyed. Before the day was done, both west side grain elevators were destroyed as well as the immigration and customs buildings. Piers 8 through 14 were severely damaged. In all, a cattle shed, fertilizer plant, and numerous CPR railcars were destroyed as well as a number of homes on Protection Street near the elevators. CP and the Harbour Board did eventually rebuild the grain elevators and the west side wharfs did return to grain export prominence.

While the grain fire of 1931 seemed like a major setback in the port's position as the number one Canadian east coast shipping port, authors David Goss and Fred Miller in their book *Saint John West and Its Neighbours*, point out that the rebuilding by the National Harbours Board provided plenty of work for west siders feeling the pinch of the Depression.

Saint John Harbour, c1900

This photo is looking from the city to West Saint John and the first CP grain elevator at Sand Point. This elevator and most of the pier infrastructure would be destroyed in the great west side port fire of 1931. In 1900, when this Isaac Erb photograph was taken, the harbour was booming especially in winter when the port of Montreal closed down and the CPR hauled grain along the Short Line to awaiting ships at Sand Point and Rodney Wharf piers. Saint John's main winter competition was Portland Maine where the Grand Trunk Railway had a rival line from Montreal that brought Canadian wheat from the west to be exported from New England. But Saint John politicians including the powerful Andrew G. Blair had fought hard for Canadian wheat to be shipped through Canadian ports.

A.G. Blair had been one of New Brunswick's most successful 19th premiers when he entered federal politics as minister of railways and canals in the Laurier Liberal government. As the minister responsible for railways and later as chairman of the federal board of railway commissioners, Blair skillfully fought the Grand Trunk's monopoly on Canadian winter grain shipments through an American port. In the mid 1990s, a number of Saint John business and political figures including Blair managed to convince Montreal's Beaver Line to call on Saint John during the winter months. This was the beginning of the port's second golden age of shipping whereby timber was replaced by prairie grain. And by 1910, Saint John was Canada's second busiest port, only trailing Montreal in volume of trade tonnage.

Steamships at Berth, West Saint John Harbour, c1900

After Canadian Pacific opened its Short Line from Montreal to Saint John, it controlled trackage only as far as the Reversing Falls. CP was interested in the little 3-mile Carleton Branch Railway that linked the short line to the Sand Point piers shown here in this Isaac Erb photograph. The line had become part of the Saint John and Maine Railway in 1880 and was acquired by the federal government in 1885. But in the 1880s, little development had occurred on the west side waterfront and while the Dominion government refused to develop Sand Point, it did agree to transfer the Carleton Branch line to the city.

CP President William Van Horne promised to invest in Sand Point if given the Carleton Branch. The wharfs would be "put into shape," he promised, with "the necessary wharves repaired and made ready for the import and export trade." Saint John Common Council readily agreed to the transfer and true to his word, Van Horne erected two state-of-the art piers at Sand Point. Later, CP and the city cost-shared the erection of the city's first grain elevator and with these co-operative agreements, the port of Saint John became Canada's major Winter Port in 1895.

Steamer Prince Rupert on the Saint John—Digby Run, c1905

The Dominion Atlantic Railway had been constructed in the 19th century through the Annapolis Valley connecting Halifax with Yarmouth where a steamer service was available to Boston. The DAR also operated a steamer passenger and freight service between Digby and Saint John that sailed the 40-mile Bay of Fundy voyage daily. The *Prince Rupert* was a 21-knot steam paddle wheeler that the DAR launched in 1895 to try and capture more of the Saint-John Digby ferry business in competition with the Yarmouth Steamship Company. The DAR was successful in driving the Yarmouth company out of Digby, and while the *Prince Rupert* did not ferry rail cars across Fundy Bay, it did interconnect with the CPR at the Sand Point pier in West Saint John. This allowed for the transporting of passengers and bulk cargo to the railway station at Digby where connections into Yarmouth and Halifax were readily available.

The CPR was especially interested in this railway with links to the port of Halifax and in 1912, acquired the Dominion Atlantic Railway in a long-term lease agreement upgrading both the Digby ferry service and the railway line, although the Yarmouth-Boston steam service was acquired by the American Eastern S.S. Corporation. During World War I, Digby's premier resort, The Pines, went bankrupt due to the wartime collapse of the tourist trade, and Canadian Pacific purchased the hotel. After extensive renovations, CP reopened the popular resort as well as the Cornwallis Inn in Kentville and expanded their tourism-railway trade throughout western Nova Scotia.

Long Wharf, Saint John Waterfront, c1900

Long Wharf is shown jutting out into the harbour in this Isaac Erb photograph. Market Slip is on the left behind Long Wharf, and across the harbour on the right can be seen the CPR grain elevator near Sand Point in West Saint John. The harbour ferry can be seen steaming from Rodney Slip to downtown Saint John. The railway trestle had been constructed from the railway bridge at the Reversing Falls across to the ICR Station in 1885, finally completing the rail connections that allow passengers and freight to travel through from Halifax and Moncton to Maine and Montreal. Long Wharf was Saint John's premier historic wharf, and while the ICR had a railway trestle operating along the wharf, CPR also had running rights through much of ICR's trackage about the harbour. CPR had acquired the St. John Bridge and Railway Extension Company through a stock purchase in 1905, and ended up controlling the trackage seen here in front of Long Wharf.

Connections to Union Station were just a few blocks outside of this photograph on the left. Tensions throughout Saint John Harbour between railway rivals ICR and CPR were evident from CPR's arrival in Saint John in 1889 up to World War II. CPR controlled lines in and out of West Saint John while the ICR operated on the east side but issues around running rights and sharing Union Station were never far from flaring up as well as the always contentious questions over who would pay for harbour improvements.

Moving Potatoes by Sleigh at Bristol, c1920

Brothers-in-law Dave Fulton and Tom Darkis are shown on the potato sleigh. The railway had come to Bristol in the late 1870s and potatoes began to be exported by freight cars shortly after. There was no heat or insulation in traditional freight cars, and so Bristol men often travelled as caretakers of potato car shipments in winter. The potatoes were loaded onto cars in bulk and partitions were erected on both sides of the doors. A sheet iron stove would be installed and fired up with a stove pipe running up along one of the doors to the outside. While the potato caretaker's job was to tend fires, they usually spent much of the time in the caboose.

Stops would be made periodically to load wood and replenish fires ensuring that the produce would not freeze in the cold Canadian winter during transportation. Once the potatoes were delivered, the caretaker would return to Bristol on the next passenger train. Without northern connections to the St. Lawrence, most of CP's passenger train traffic from Bristol was headed south even if the final destination was Montreal. After the CPP took over the New Brunswick Railway in 1889, a daily 4:00 pm express left Bristol for McAdam arriving in time for a hot evening meal at the station before heading out on an overnighter that offered sleeping arrangements, guaranteeing the passenger a good night sleep before arriving at Montreal's Grand Central Station at eight the following morning.

Railway Bridge, Grand Falls, c1895

This George Taylor photograph shows the old railway bridge at the back of the photo. In 1896, the bridge was damaged by frost and taken out of service since the structure was deemed too fragile to support train traffic. Attempts were made by Canadian Pacific (they had taken over operations from the New Brunswick Railway in 1889) to repair the damage but in 1900, the bridge collapsed and had to be rebuilt. Grand Falls was incorporated in 1890 after the name was changed from Colebrooke. The largest waterfalls in the Maritimes falls 23 metres over a series of rock ledges, and the first bridge over the St. John River at the falls was a suspension bridge erected in 1860.

The bridge opened with a warning overhead: "walk your horse or fine of $20." The St. Andrews and Quebec Railway (renamed the New Brunswick and Canada Railway) had reached Grand Falls in 1877 where a roundhouse and bridge were constructed. This line had started at Passamaquoddy Bay several decades earlier before going bankrupt after reaching Woodstock in the 1860s. The New Brunswick Railway under Alexander Gibson's direction had built from Fredericton's north side to Woodstock where the two lines joined going north to Grand Falls and Edmundston. In 1882, the New Brunswick and Canada Railway was leased to the New Brunswick Railway and then became part of the CPR.

Old Edmundston Ferry, c1910

This Isaac Erb photo shows the cable ferry over the St. John River at Edmundston from the New Brunswick side with the Maine shore in the background. Two roads are seen leading away from the river. This old ferry still provided service for residents until the International Bridge was constructed in the 1920s. Around 1900, the Bangor and Aroostock Railway still ended at Caribou, and so all goods destined for Madawaska and northern Maine came up the St. John River via the CPR, overland from Rivière-du-Loup through the Temiscouata Railway, or later along the International Railway from Campbellton.

Once the National Transcontinental Railway came through in 1912, Edmundston had a direct service north to Quebec City, and south through Central New Brunswick to Moncton. When the bridge was finally constructed across the St. John River, Canadian railways could then connect with the Bangor and Aroostook Railway coming in from Maine. During this time, goods destined for Maine were inspected by a single US customs inspector at Edmundston. The inspector was not always diligent in customs matters and consequently, Madawaska County became known as wide-open territory with smuggling kingpin Joe Walnut firmly entrenched at his Brunswick Hotel headquarters in St. Leonard.

SAINT JOHN'S
BRIDGES, FERRIES,
& STREET RAILWAY

Railway Bridge at Reversing Falls, Suspension Bridge in Background, Saint John, c1890

The camera is pointed east towards the city while a St. John River Woodboat is passing underneath. After the European and North American Railway from Shediac to Saint John was completed in 1860, the Western Extension Railway was built from a point near the Reversing Falls in West Saint John into Maine. Yet the problem remained that a horse and wagon ride across the Suspension Bridge or a ferry across Saint John Harbour was still necessary in order for passengers to travel across to Saint John and connect to the ICR. The Carleton Branch Railway had already been built in 1871 from the Reversing Falls to the Fairville station in West Saint John where a ferry connected into downtown. But a railway bridge across the gorge at Reversing Falls was considered essential and in 1881, a bill to incorporate the St. John Bridge and Railway Company was passed in the provincial legislature. The goal was to build a bridge across the St.

John River and lay tracks connecting to the ICR line that ended at the Intercolonial Station on Mill Street in Saint John. It took four years to build but in 1885, a cantilever type railway bridge was completed over Reversing Falls parallel to the old suspension bridge. The ensuing tracks finally allowed freight and passengers from eastern New Brunswick to travel through to the United States without having to take a ferry across the harbour.

Three Bridges at Reversing Falls, Saint John, c1915

This photograph was taken looking over the Reversing Falls Bridges towards Saint John Harbour with Navy Island in the middle of the harbour, West Saint John on the right, and east Saint John in the background. The Railway Bridge is on the left with the Road Bridge in the Middle and the old Suspension Bridge on the right. A rare view since all three bridges only remained in place for a short time. The Suspension Bridge was originally erected in 1854 as the only toll bridge in the province until the city made passage free in the 1870s. It was a wooden-planked affair with large overhead cables that were anchored in the rocky banks but the Suspension Bridge was essentially a foot-bridge unable to support heavy trolley traffic.

The railway structure on the left was built in 1885, finally allowing rail service to pass directly through Saint John. Once automobiles became common in the early 1900s, the road bridge in the centre of the photo was constructed and until the 1940s, also carried a streetcar back and forth across the falls. The road bridge stills stands today but the old Suspension Bridge was torn down in 1916. The bridges at Reversing Falls as well as regular ferry service across the harbour did much to stimulate business and communication between the communities around Saint John Harbour.

Second Railway Bridge Over Reversing Falls, Saint John, c1925

This Issac Erb photo was taken from the upriver side of the falls showing a CPR train crossing the bridge. The highway bridge over the falls is slightly visible behind the bridge towards the city but the old Suspension Bridge is long gone. Saint John's first Railway Bridge had served the railway industry well for 35 years but after World War I, Canadian Pacific's trains had become much heavier and the old cantilever style bridge was deemed fragile and unsafe. A new low-trestle railway bridge was begun in 1920 north of the original bridge and opened for traffic the following year. The old abutments from the original bridge can still be seen sticking out of the rocks at the falls. The new structure featured a similar cantilever-type bridge but was much stronger in building supports and remains in service today, almost ninety years later.

Railway Ferry Dock, Saint John, c1880

This photo shows the harbour ferry making connections with a train. Saint Johners had had harbour ferry service beginning in Loyalist times from the west side at Rodney Wharf to city centre but the coming of the railway complicated the service. The tiny Carleton Branch Railway was built by a group of West Saint John businessmen to connect the Western Extension Railway that had ended near the Reversing Falls with the west side docks. Until the railway bridge was finished over Reversing Falls in 1885, railway passengers coming in to Saint John from western New Brunswick could take a horse and wagon ride over the Suspension Bridge at Reversing Falls but the more popular option was to continue in by rail to the west side pier, and hop a ferry into Saint John.

But after 1885, passengers as well as freight coming in on CP's line from McAdam could pass directly over the Reversing Falls Railway Bridge to Union Station and downtown Saint John. This new situation left the harbour ferry service downgraded and forced to resume its' pre-railway status as strictly catering to west siders coming into the city. And this loss of business in the late 1880s left Common Council with some lively debates over the future of the service. In the end, council agreed to spend additional financial resources that saw the ferry service upgraded in the early 1900s with the launching of the modern steel vessels *Ludlow* and *Governor Carleton*.

Military Parade and Streetcars, Dock Street, Saint John, c1914

In the early 1900s, Saint John was the major industrial centre of New Brunswick with a strong union tradition dating well back to the 1840s. But the militant labour groups of the early 20th century were much better organized, affiliated with powerful international organizations, and less afraid to confront employers with strikes. Violence and lockouts became common bargaining techniques of the period and longshoremen, carpenters, textile workers, printers, even police officers formed union brotherhoods to further their interests. The most violent union confrontation in New Brunswick's history occurred in 1914, when a dispute between the St. John Railway Company and its workers erupted into a bloody riot. The Saint John Street Railway Company had been first formed as the horse-drawn Peoples Street Railway Company in 1866. In 1886, an electric streetcar company was formed and it was still a private syndicate prior to World War 1 when its workers formed Local No. 663 of the Amalgamated Association of Street and Electric Railway Employees.

After the local demanded an eight-hour working day, company officials rejected the request, and hired private detectives to spy on the union. Union leaders were soon dismissed on trumped-up charges as the company discarded a conciliation board's recommendations and ignored the worker's decision to prepare for a strike. At a meeting at the Odd Fellows Hall on Union Street, the street railway workers voted to strike and with full public sympathy, the workers issued a memo that they would be willing to "fight this matter out in St. John for years if necessary." Strike-breakers arrived from Montreal and on July 23, a confrontation became inevitable as striking workers in their colourful blue uniforms and their large group of supporters took to the streets of Saint John. Accompanied by the Carleton Cornet Band and carrying in scripted banners that declared "We Are Fighting For Freedom" and "We Will Walk", the railwaymen marched through the working-class district of the north end while thousands of onlookers cheered.

Thousands more were on hand as gangs of strike-breakers roamed the city intimidating the strikers. With an estimated eight thousand people cheering the marching strikers, the mob of workers began to take complete control of the streets. The police force was soon overwhelmed and unable to prevent the crowd from stopping the trolleys. Finally exasperated, the military was called in as Mayor James Frink stood at the S.P.C.A. fountain at Market Square and read the riot act to the swarming crowd. The Mayor noted that both rioters and onlookers could be imprisoned for life if they disobeyed his command to disperse. The mob seem to calm down with the threat of life imprisonment but panic broke out as Lieutenant Hubert Stethem and his Royal Canadian Dragoons suddenly charged down King Street on horseback with swords slashing, knocking down men, women, and children. The crowd reacted to the cavalry charge by fighting

Saint John Street Railway Employees, Tug-of-War Team, c1905

back. Lieutenant Stethem's face was smashed with a flying bottle while another trooper was knocked from his horse. Knives were drawn, and rioters slashed at troopers and horses. The troopers retreated but more violence erupted as stalled streetcars were overturned and set ablaze. The railway company's powerhouse was attacked and shut down, but private detectives defended the repair barn and the mob was turned away with flying buckshot. The next day Saint John's streets were littered with overturned trolleys and broken glass.

The Saint John Globe newspaper reported the following "The affair is the most disgraceful, the most regrettable that has occurred in St. John in the lifetime of the present generation." City officials attempted to break the stalemate between the union and the company. Peace was restored when suspended union leader Fred Ramsay accepted a lifetime position with the city's public works department, and the remaining dismissed workers were reinstated. Normal streetcar service was resumed a day later. While tensions remained high between the union and the St. John Railway Company, war with Germany was declared in August, and most unions temporally suspended their militancy to assist the Canadian war effort. And while the call to serve in Canada's military effort overseas did much to disperse labour agitation in Saint John, union militancy appeared again in the 1920s as the New Brunswick economy began to deteriorate under the strain of inflation and the postwar recession.

NEW BRUNSWICK
CENTRAL RAILWAY

Locomotive Delivering Coal, Norton, c1900

The old No. 5 locomotive is shown at Norton Station hauling coal and featuring the American standard wheel alignment (4-4-0). Norton was the
southern terminus for the New Brunswick Central Railway that first opened in
1888 between Norton and Chipman. The Central Railway Company's grand
plan was to construct a railway between Gibson on the north side of Fredericton
and the ICR running between Saint John and Shediac. As early as 1873, company directors were interested in the Newcastle coal fields at Minto as potential
cargo but they also knew lumber mills could benefit from a railway line through
central New Brunswick. In 1884, the decision was made to proceed with the

line a distance of 80 miles from the coalfields at the head of Grand Lake across the Salmon River, past Chipman, Johnston, and Watertown, to connect with the ICR at Norton. The New Brunswick Central Railway Company featured a who's who of prominent businessmen from central New Brunswick including Alexander Gibson, George E. King, Frederick P. Thompson, Alexander Stirling, and Charles Burpee. Egerton R. Burpee was chief engineer and the province offered a subsidy of $6,200 per mile. Contractors were hired in December 1886, including railway builder John Killam, and work was first carried out throughout the winter of 1887.

NB Central Railway Train Unloading Logs at Pennlyn, c1905

Building the southeast end of the New Brunswick Central Railway between Norton and Grand Lake took place throughout 1887 and involved a number of crews working at different places. One report in early 1887 cited 800 men at work including a crew cutting through rock near Norton, a second crew at work further north at Belleisle Creek, and a third working party cutting at Salmon Creek. At the same time, a bridge was being erected at Armstrong Point in the Washademoak Lake area. By early 1888, the line had been graded, five stations erected, four water tanks installed, plus a significant amount of rolling stock had arrived. The railway opened the same year and featured 20 flat cars and two locomotives, including one that had been built at Fleming's Foundry in Saint John. The second locomotive had been purchased from the Rome Locomotive

Works in New York State and shipped by scow up the St. John River where it was off loaded at Chipman. Yet the province had only agreed to a building subsidy between Norton and Chipman. But the company immediately began to lobby the government to provide an additional subsidy to assist building the line further west from Chipman to the Newcastle coalfields at Minto.

The company argued that the line would then be extended all the way to Gibson across the river from Fredericton. In 1894, the province did contribute $48,000 to help build the railway the further 15 miles into the coal fields but after 1895, New Brunswick would not commit additional funds to assist the company extend the line towards Fredericton. And another two decades would go by before the railway was completed to the banks of the St. John River at Gibson.

CP Locomotive No. 7078 Dumping Fill at Bettinson's Bridge near Belleisle Station, c1921

This railway had been constructed as the New Brunswick Central Railway in 1888 and built in stages between Norton and Gibson on the north side of Fredericton. Before the CPR took over the line, the Central Railway had seven small steam locomotives in service including five engines built in the US, and two locomotives that were acquired from the Fleming Foundry in Saint John. Most of the engines were configured in the American standard wheel arrangement 4-4-0 but two locomotives had a 4-6-0 alignment.

The entire line was laid in 52 and 56 pound steel rails. Rail width was standard gauge because by the 1880s, the question of rail gauge had been settled— North America was essentially standard gauge territory with a few exceptions for mountain lines and timber spurs. As can be seen from the photograph of the wooden trestles, the New Brunswick Central Railway was built a bit on the cheap side. The bridges and rough terrain sections were not supported with extensive iron supports nor was extra ballast laid. After Canadian Pacific took over the entire railway between 1910 and 1912, they began to use their own locomotives but found most too heavy to run over the fragile bridges. But of the five old Central engines used on the line, No.29, 30, 105, 136, and 144, three are still in existence as historic museum pieces including old No.29 that attracts tourists in Albert County as part of the Salem and Hillsborough Railway. And in 1958, the CP section of the old Central Railway could boost having the oldest steam locomotive in service in Canada. Old No.136 was still engaged in moving freight until it was retired later the same year.

Grand Lake Coal and Railway Station, Minto, c1908

This station was built in 1904 and is today a museum featuring Grand Lake railway and coal mining history. In 1894, the New Brunswick Central Railway line from Norton to Chipman had been extended to Minto and the portion west of Chipman had been incorporated as the New Brunswick Coal and Railway Company. This section between Chipman and Minto became known as the Grand Lake Coal Railway since until 1912, the line ended at Minto where coal shipments were transported southeast to connect with the ICR at Norton. After Canadian Pacific became involved as operator in 1910, the railway was extended towards Fredericton and the railway was called the Fredericton and Grand Lake Coal and Railway Company. Provincial and federal subsidies essentially built the line from Minto to Fredericton North and CPR controlled the line through a series of long-term leases.

During World War I, coal from Minto was moved west through Fredericton as well as southeast to the ICR line that connected with Moncton and Saint John. Yet the railway had not been built to the highest standards and much of the CPR's rolling stock was too heavy to run over a number of the old wooden structures. Some rebuilding did occur especially during World War II, but the section between Norton and Pennlyn was abandoned in 1961, cutting the line off from its southern terminus. The Salmon River Bridge at Chipman was declared unsafe about 1972 but coal still moved west by rail until the 1980s when the entire New Brunswick Central Railway line was closed.

CP Locomotive No. 84 on the Right, Chipman, c1912

This photo shows the old New Brunswick Coal and Railway line running through Chipman in 1912 but around the same time, the line had been taken over by the CPR. And behind the line, a new railroad, the National Transcontinental Railway, is under construction. A third national railway line through New Brunswick was controversial since both the ICR and the CPR were not booming rail lines in the early 1900s. Yet the NTR was a rare creature, a straight-as-a-bullet through the province, and very efficient in moving freight in and out of New Brunswick. As well, the NTR was a boost to central New Brunswick. Both McGivney Station and Chipman, where the Canada Eastern (part of ICR) and the Central New Brunswick Railway (CPR), intersected the NTR, and both communities benefited from moving freight fast and efficiently. Yet the NTR was a government funded and operated rail line, identical to the ICR, and both railways hurt the CPR's business by undercutting freight rates and competing for new business throughout eastern Canada.

The upshot of the NTR entering the central New Brunswick railway market was that the CPR, while allowed to take over the Central New Brunswick Railway between Norton and Fredericton North, did not see a great future in the line. There was now too much trackage and the financial commitment to undertake major upgrades would not be made by Canadian Pacific. Thus the Central line was never able to compete successfully with the two public railways even after the NTR-ICR lines were merged into the Canadian National Railway.

Locomotive Taking Water at Perry near Minto, c1953

This Canadian Pacific No.29 steam engine (4-4-0) worked the Central New Brunswick line between Norton and Chipman in the early days of the rail line. The old No.29 was one of the original seven locomotives that hauled freight on the railway and was reluctantly maintained by the CPR after it took over the line in 1912. CP's big freight engines were deemed too heavy to cross the fragile wooden bridges along the railway. The No. 29 engine actively worked until 1961 when sections of the southern line were abandoned due to safety issues as well as a lack of freight. Today, the No.29 is still somewhat operational and sits at Hillsborough as part of the historic Salem and Hillsborough Railway. Two other steam engines from the old days of the Central New Brunswick Railway are also preserved and on display as museum artifacts near Toronto (No.136) and Quebec (No.144).

Railway Wreck, Central New Brunswick Railway, Wasson's Brook, July 12, 1902

The railway line from Chipman to Norton crossed over difficult terrain and the Central New Brunswick Railway Company was not well financed when the line was erected in the late 1880s. Consequently, a number of serious accidents occurred including this train at Wasson's Brook in 1902 when a brush fire burned the wooden bridge. The locomotive was charging along the line unaware of the collapse and fell into the brook, killing the engineer W. Nodwell. This photo shows the mangled wreck of the engine and freight cars in the brook with a number of rescue workers accessing the damage. Other train wrecks seemed to mirror the Wasson's Brook accident since wooden trestles and bridge spans would often give way due to faulty workmanship on the original construction.

In August 1900, a train collapsed on Sargeson's Bridge near Cumberland Bay, falling through the defective bridge trestles. Another engineer, John Duncan was killed and two years later, a span of Cody's Bridge over Washademoak Lake gave way, and a locomotive plus two freight cars plunged into the lake. The train fireman Stanley Brand was lost in the Cody's Bridge accident and the railway was closed below Chipman for a period of seven months until the bridge was repaired. Unfortunately, the company was not willing or unable to radically overhaul many of the bridge supporters along the line and a number of other accidents took place.

Collapse of Cody's Bridge, Train in Washademoak Lake, 1902

St. Martins Railway Station, St. Martins, c1900

This photo shows the little railway station on Beach Street with the railway tracks and shoreline in the foreground. While the station was the terminus of the line at St. Martins, the manually operated turntable where the locomotives would turn is not showed in this photograph. The St. Martins Railway Company was first incorporated in 1871 as the St. Martins and Upham Railway Company. The railway was constructed to connect the flourishing shipbuilding village of St. Martins with the Upham Valley, ending at Hampton where the European and North American Railway ran between Saint John and Shediac. With a $5,000 per mile provincial government subsidy, the little railway broke ground in 1874 and opened in 1878, after costing the province $112,000 and the company only $15,000. Yet the railway struggled to operate profitably from the outset, and after ten years of negative cash flow, the line was taken over by the Central Railway, becoming its Southern Division. Yet the Central Railway was equally unable to make the line work, mainly due to a lack of traffic. The line rarely operated in winter since it lacked snow removable equipment.

In 1897, the line was returned to its original shareholders and renamed the Hampton and Saint Martins Railway. In 1906, the line was sold to new operators at a big loss and then named the St. Martins Railway. But no one could make the line work profitably. No matter how many times new owners tried to cut costs and boost revenue, there was simply too little freight or passengers to move along the line. At the end of World War I, the federal government was buying private railways throughout eastern Canada and offered $65,000 for the St. Martins Railway. The company jumped at the offer and the line was folded into the Canadian Government Railways and became part of the CNR. Canadian National was also unable to make the little line a going concern and in 1940, the line was abandoned completely.

American Standard Locomotive, St. Martins Railway, c1897

A Hampton-St. Martins sign is visible on the coal car behind the man with the bicycle on the far right. The St. Martins Railway operated on a shoe-string budget and even had to borrow or rent rolling stock from the ICR in order to move traffic from time to time. The little railway only had two locomotives and they often broke down. This one featured the American standard wheel configuration of 4-4-0, meaning four guiding (leading) wheels, four driving wheels and zero trailing wheels comprising the wheel alignment of the engine. Steam locomotives throughout North America were identified by their wheel configuration including the number of wheels, and while there were many different wheel systems in place over the years, the 4-4-0 proved to be the most popular.

Developed in the 1840s, the American standard locomotive wheel system became in high demand in the 1850s. It proved so flexible in adapting to new engine technology that the CPR still employed this wheel arrangement in New Brunswick in the 1960s even after the average locomotive weight had doubled to about 25 tons. While not an ideal choice for special tasks such as climbing mountain passes, the 4-4-0 proved an excellent wheel system for pulling freight or passenger cars. This was because the guiding wheels included a stabilizing beam connecting to the driving wheels allowing for flexibility and yet stability in negotiating rough or sloping track. The early American standard engines had short steam boilers, low drivers, and tight spacing along the driving wheels and yet as larger engines with extensive innovations were developed, the 4-4-0 arrangement proved to be still capable of maintaining strong performance over the approximately 120 year life-span of the steam locomotive.

NATIONAL
TRANSCONTINENTAL RAILWAY
& THE VALLEY LINE

McGivney Junction, National Transcontinental Railway, c1912

Three sets of tracks are shown here, one coming in from the left side to merge with the trunk line while a second line on the right is shown intersecting the main line in the background near the tower. By the early 1900s, there were essentially two railways operating in New Brunswick. The privately run Canadian Pacific operating in western New Brunswick and the public owned and operated Intercolonial Railway in the east and north. Small branch lines did continue to operate but they would soon be bought and merged into the ICR. The idea that another national public railway was needed in Canada did not originate in New Brunswick nor did the other two railways agree with the notion. But with significant development on the Prairies through to the Pacific coast, it was deemed necessary by the federal government to build another transcontinental railway north of the CPR. Rather than patching together existing rail lines and building new tracks—a mere thousand miles over the Canadian Shield above the CPR line along Lake Superior—Sir Wilfred Laurier and his Liberal government chose to build an entirely new railway through northern Ontario to Winnipeg, Edmonton, and Prince Rupert. Politics made it necessary to extend the line to Quebec City, and once this was announced, New Brunswick demanded the NTR be extended to Moncton.

When completed in 1912, the National Transcontinental Railway measured 2019 miles from Moncton to Winnipeg alone, and while Laurier had originally budgeted 13 million for construction, the Moncton to Winnipeg section ended up costing Canadian taxpayers 161 million. The 250 miles through New Brunswick ran from Moncton straight to Chipman, north to McGivney, Napadogan, Juniper, Plaster Rock, Grand Falls, and Edmundston before heading west past Baker Lake and into Charny, and Quebec City. While the cost was enormous, the line ran relatively straight through New Brunswick but the problem was that a third transcontinental rail network was not needed in 1912, especially not in eastern Canada. The NTR operator in the east, the Grand Trunk, reneged on its operating contract and the federal government then formed the Canadian Government Railways mainly to operate the NTR. But soon, more railways were in trouble including the Canadian Northern Railway, and after World War I, Canadian National Railway was formed to manage and operate Canada's vast public national rail system. And during the 1920s, the CNR became the operator of both the NTR and the ICR. And a number of railway historians are convinced that this forced merger was the result of the reckless construction of the NTR into eastern Canada.

Building the National Transcontinental Railway, Hardwood Ridge, near Minto, c1910

Unlike the Intercolonial Railway, the National Transcontinental Railway was built in the straightest way possible to move goods and passengers from Moncton to Upper Canada. The NTR intersected a number of New Brunswick branch railways including the New Brunswick Coal and Railway at Chipman, the Canadian Eastern Railway at McGivney, and the Tobique Valley Railway at Plaster Rock. While the new railway did create some new business and captured some traffic from the ICR and the CPR, the line was certainly not economical and seemed to almost bump into the other railways.

At Pacific Junction west of Moncton, the NTR and ICR shadowed each other so close on route into Moncton that near the entrance to Killam Drive on the outskirts of the city, the point across from the old Poor House became known as "shake hands" by the railway engineers. Yet for all this duplication, when CN took over the two lines, they considered the NTR route superior to the old ICR route, and adopted the NTR line for much of their fast-freight shipments. Even the shake-hands section west to Pacific Junction was reduced to one line in the 1930s and the NTR route became the CNR's trunk line out of Moncton while the old ICR line was torn up and became a straight-as-an-arrow highway taking motor traffic west to the Trans Canada Highway.

NTR Employees at Sunbury, Near Hardwood Ridge, c1912

Railway crews had hard lives in the early years of the railway. Most freight trains required at least six men and a typical freight train had a locomotive engineer, fireman, conductor, and at least three brakemen. Most operating crews would run back and forth over what was called "division points" usually about 100 miles, for example between Moncton and Saint John. Crews were usually assigned to a locomotive and endeavoured to safeguard their rig over their division. The engineer was the one with the steam power in his hand and like a ship's captain, took personal pride in keeping his locomotive in top working order. Passenger trains were especially clean and shinning in order to encourage the public to travel by train. A fireman on a steam locomotive was responsible for maintaining safety since boiler fires and explosions were all too common. The conductor maintained the back end of a train and also dealt with the paying public on passenger trains, managing the stops and maintaining order. Brakemen had very demanding jobs especially as trains became longer in attempting to haul more freight. Initially, steam engines were controlled and stopped by engine brakes but eventually freight and passenger cars were equipped with manual brakes. Brakemen would then need to hustle from car to car, setting and releasing the brakes according to the whistle signals from the engineer. Passenger cars usually had brakes at the back but often freight cars required brakemen to walk on top of the moving train—regardless of the weather—in order to set the brakes. This required extreme dexterity jumping between moving cars. Unfortunately, brakemen often suffered tragic deaths by falling off moving trains. Eventually, automatic breaking systems were installed on the newer diesel and electric trains, making a brakeman's working life a lot safer.

Building the Valley Railway, Island View, c1912

A steam shovel is excavating for the Saint John and Quebec Railway at Island View above Fredericton. The idea of a railway from Saint John up the St. John River Valley to Quebec was one of the early railway proposals put forward by railway promoters in the 1840s. Yet no railroad had proceeded along the valley during the heyday of railway construction. The National Transcontinental through New Brunswick was announced in 1908 but the problem was this publicly constructed railway would bypass the valley going directly from Edmundston to Grand Falls, Chipman, and on to Moncton.

Bypassing the St. John River Valley was not good valley politics, and pressure mounted to address this historic wrong. A $15,000 per mile subsidy was announced by Premier Pugsley to anyone willing to build a railway 250 miles from Saint John to connect with the NTR at Grand Falls. When the subsidy was sweetened to $25,000 a mile, Maine Senator Arthur Gould, owner of the Aroostook Valley Railroad, incorporated the Saint John and Quebec Railway and broke ground on the line that was surveyed to run from Fredericton to Pokiok, and on to Woodstock.

Railway Station, Gagetown, Valley Railway, c1930

Construction of the Saint John and Quebec Railway began in 1911 and by the end of 1914, with a provincial subsidy sweetened to $35,000 a mile, 120 miles of work had been completed. The line extended from Westfield to Gagetown, Fredericton, and northwest along the St. John River Valley to Centreville. Premier J. Kidd Flemming had assumed power in New Brunswick in 1912 and with his power base in Hartland, was anxious to have the valley line completed. Yet Flemming's fortunes were shattered when he was found guilty of accepting money for his party's campaign fund from Valley Railway contractors including Maine Senator Gould who paid Flemming's party at least $100,000.

Construction beyond Centreville was suspended and the federal government eventually assumed responsibility for operating the service between Saint John and Centreville. Below Westfield, running rights in to Saint John was acquired from the CPR and although the line along the valley to Fredericton was 20 miles longer than the CPR line, the Valley Railway continued to operate during the 1920s. And above Fredericton, the valley line was patched together to Grand Falls but measured an additional 50 miles against the well-established CPR line. In 1929, the CNR purchased the valley line for six million dollars and incorporated the railway into their system. With little traffic and numerous rail lines operating nearby, the Valley Railway stopped all passenger traffic in 1952. After the Mactaquac Dam opened in 1867, rail service between Fredericton and Woodstock was permanently discontinued.

Westfield Beach Station, Valley Railway, c1920

When the Dominion government announced a third transcontinental railway to be built across Canada in 1908, Saint John lobbied hard to have the Atlantic terminal of the National Transcontinental Railway located at Courtenay Bay. When the route was chosen to proceed from Grand Falls directly through to Moncton via McGivney and Chipman, Saint John still managed to convinced all levels of government to help build a valley railway from Saint John north to Grand Falls to connect with the NTR. The merchants and local officials in Saint John saw a historic opportunity to open up Courtenay Bay to development including shipbuilding, a dry dock, and a rail terminal. But the problem became convincing the federal and provincial governments to chip in to build the valley line down the east side of the lower St. John River.

Bridges were especially expensive to build in the early 1900s, and to enter the city from the Kingston Peninsula or Gondola Point meant extensive bridge construction. In the end, World War I, a provincial government scandal, and the collapse of the Grand Trunk-federal government deal to operate the NTR, all conspired to halt the Valley Railway at Westfield on the west side of the St. John River. Running rights were acquired from the CPR to enter the west side of the city and Saint John's hopes to develop Courtenay Bay would have to wait for a more opportune time. Once the federal government's ICR assumed responsibility for operating the NTR, the Valley Railway was considered largely redundant especially above Fredericton since freight coming out of Saint John could easily be connected into the NTR through the ICR's Fredericton-McGivney line.

RAILWAY TIMELINE

1796 Frenchman Nicholas-Joseph Cugnot builds the first steam-propelled wagon.

1804 Englishman Richard Trevithick develops a full-size, high-pressure locomotive called the *Pen-y-Darran* engine.

1825 George Stephenson launches the Stockton & Darlington Railway using steam-powered engines. Stephenson also develops the first modern public steam railway, the Liverpool and Manchester Railway.

1827 St. Andrews entrepreneurs first approach British authorities for assistance to build a railway to Quebec. They are turned down.

1828 American Horatio Allen launches his *Stourbridge Lion* steam engine on the Delaware & Hudson railway line in Pennsylvania. The locomotive proves too heavy for the light tracks.

1829 Robert Stephenson's fast engine, the *Rocket*, wins the Rainhill tram trials with a top speed of 29 mph and becomes the standard British engine design. The same year, the steam engine *Tom Thumb* debuts on the Baltimore and Ohio Railway.

1835 The St. Andrews and Quebec Railway Company is formed.

1836 British North America's first railway, the Champlain & St. Lawrence Railway, opens in Montreal.

1837 British officer Captain Yule surveys a railway line from Point Lévis opposite Quebec, to Saint Andrews. Much of the territory encompassing the line is in dispute and will be awarded to Maine.

1839 The first steam locomotive in North America to burn coal and run over all-metal rails, the 15-metric ton *Samson*, transports coal for the Stellarton Albion Mines in Nova Scotia's Pictou County.

1847 The St. Andrews and Quebec Railway Company, with some British capital, and provincial support, breaks ground toward Quebec but soon runs into financial difficulties.

1850 A new railway line is surveyed from St. Andrews to Richmond Corner near Woodstock. A locomotive, *Pioneer*, is ordered from Wales at a cost of $5,000 but by 1852, only 12 miles have been constructed.

1851 The New Brunswick Legislature passes a bill with a $250,000 subsidy incorporating the European and North American Railway to be built between Bangor and Halifax, significantly cutting shipping times on the North Atlantic. British officials refused to support the project.

1853 The Atlantic & St. Lawrence Railway opens its Montreal to Portland Maine rail line. Construction begins at Shediac and Saint John on the European and North American Railway.

1855 The first section of the Nova Scotia Railway from Richmond in Halifax's north end to Lower Sackville opens. Soon the line is extended to Truro and at Windsor Junction, a thirty-two mile branch line is constructed to Windsor.

1856 The Grand Trunk Railway opens between Montreal and Toronto.

1857 New financing and a new name—the New Brunswick and Canada Railway Company —allows construction to proceed from St. Andrews toward Woodstock, and 34 miles of track become operational. The first two sections of the European and North American Railway opens between Moncton and Shediac, as well as between Saint John and Coldbrook.

1858 The Phoenix Foundry in Saint John builds the famous *Loostack* and *Ossekeag* steam engines, the first New Brunswick built locomotives.

1860 Construction of the European and North American Railway is completed between Saint John and Shediac.

1862 The New Brunswick and Canada Railway Company is finally finished from St. Andrews to Richmond Corner. But the next year, the company defaults on its bond payment and goes into receivership.

1864 New Brunswick passes the Facility Act, nicknamed the Lobster Act, since it offered a subsidy of $10,000 per mile, encouraging railways to be built in every direction much like a lobster claw. The act also offers a bonus of $20,000 for any company connecting New Brunswick to Upper Canada by rail. But the province is broke and changes the subsidy from cash to 10,000 free acres of land per mile.

1866 The St. Stephen Branch Railway Company opens a 19-mile branch rail line from Watt Junction on the St. Andrew and Quebec Railway line into St. Stephen.

1867 Confederation of the four British North American colonies includes the promise of an Intercolonial Railway to the Maritimes. The appointment of Sir Stanford Fleming as engineer-in-chief is confirmed.

1869 Under the terms of Confederation, the European and North American Railway becomes part of the Dominion's Intercolonial Railway. The same year, the Fredericton Branch Railway connects 22 miles from the capital to Fredericton Junction, linking Fredericton with the Western Extension Railway.

1870 The Maine Central Railway (Bangor to Portland) converts to standard gauge (4 ft, 8.5 inch) making it inevitable that the Western Extension Railway would convert. They finally do but not until 1877.

1871 The Maine Western Extension line from Bangor to Vanceboro opens with US President Ulysses S. Grant undertaking a last spike ceremony. The same year, Saint John's Carleton Branch Railway links into the Western Extension Railway by building from the Reversing Falls 3.5 miles to the west side docks.

1872 A fire destroys the Shediac railway shops at the same time that an extensive push is being conducted throughout New Brunswick to complete the ICR. The railway repair centre is moved to Moncton.

1875 The ICR's final bridge is completed over the Northwest Miramichi River.

1876 The Intercolonial Railway between Halifax and Rivière-du-Loup is completed. The same year, the Albert Railway Company between Hillsborough and Salisbury opens as well as the Petitcodiac to Elgin line.

1878 Alexander Gibson opens the New Brunswick Railway built from the north side of Fredericton north to Edmundston. The same year, St. Martins and Upham Railway opens between St. Martins and Hampton.

1881 Construction begins on the Kent Northern Railway connecting Richibucto with the ICR at Kent Junction. It opens two years later.

1882 The Grand Southern Railway between St. Stephen and Saint John officially opens. Alexander Gibson's railway company is reorganized as the New Brunswick Railway Company with Gibson out. The new company acquires long-terms leases over numerous western New Brunswick branch railways including the St. Stephen Branch Railway, the St. Andrews and Quebec Railway, and the Woodstock Railway Company. It will be later revealed that the CPR is a major stockholder in the New Brunswick Railway.

1883 A group of Sackville businessmen build a branch rail line to Cape Tormentine. The first 18 miles to Baie Verte is completed in 1883 and three years later, the full 36 miles to Cape Tormentine is finished.

1884 The New Brunswick Railway consolidates their service and repair shops at McAdam Junction, closing out their facilities in St. Andrew. The same year, the ICR opens a stunning new Romanesque Revival railway station at Saint John.

1885 The Canadian Pacific Railway to the Pacific is completed. As well, a cantilever type railway bridge is built over Reversing Falls at Saint John, connecting the ICR with the Western Extension Railway to Maine.

1886 The Bouctouche and Moncton Railway, a little 32-mile rail line known locally as the B & M railway, officially opens. Also in 1886, A.E. Killam builds the Petitcodiac and Havelock Railway.

1887 The Canada Eastern Railway Company opens a line between South Devon opposite Fredericton to Chatham. One year later, the Fredericton Railway Bridge is constructed, giving the railway direct access to downtown Fredericton.

1888 The New Brunswick Central Railway opens section one of their line between Norton and Chipman.

1889 Canadian Pacific opens the Short Line, a railway to the Atlantic Coast at Saint John, completing its Canadian transcontinental railway. And for a fee of $370,000 per year, CPR acquires the many leases of the New Brunswick Railway. The same year, the Temiscouata Railway opens between Rivière-du-Loup and Edmundston. The next year the line is extended to Conners.

1890 Virtually all broad-gauged railways in North America have been converted to standard gauge in order to allow for the interchange of freight in a cost effective manner. The same year, employment at the little railway border community of McAdam jumps to 125 people.

1891 Despite having finished 19 kilometres of track at a cost of $3,500,000, Henry Ketchum's ship railway at Chignecto fails to be completed.

1893 The Canada Eastern Railway launches the *Suburban*, a shuttle train service that operates six round trips a day between Fredericton and the Marysville Cotton Mill.

1894 The New Brunswick Central Railway finally extends its line 15 miles from Chipman into the Grand Lake coal fields. This section between Chipman and Minto becomes known as the Grand Lake Coal Railway. As well, the Tobique Valley Railway opens between Plaster Rock and Perth Junction.

1895 Montreal's Beaver Line (Canadian Shipping Company) agrees to call at West Saint John during the winter months in order to ship CP's western grain overseas. Saint John is now declared Canada's Winter Port.

1897 Moncton's grand ICR Station opens.

1898 The Caraquet Railway is completed through to Shippagan.

1900 The Whyte classification system, devised by American Frederick Whyte, is adopted throughout the railway industry in North America. Steam locomotives are identified by this arrangement including the number of wheels: guide wheels at front, driving wheels in the middle, and trailing wheels at the rear. The most common arrangement is 4-4-0. The same year, the CPR Station at McAdam opens, one of the largest and most ambitious railway stations built by the CPR in eastern Canada.

1902 The Algonquin Hotel in St. Andrews is purchased by CP.

1904 CP establishes the Angus railway shops in Montreal. Over 700 locomotives will be built at Angus. The Canada Eastern Railway is sold to the federal government for $819,000. ICR announces the launch of the *Ocean Limited*, an overnight express service between Montreal and Halifax.

1905 The Intercolonial Railway takes over the Canada Eastern Railway after the federal government purchases it from Boss Gibson for $819,000. The same year, the Fredericton Railway Bridge is also taken over by the ICR.

1906 One million dollars worth of railway buildings, rolling stock, and equipment are destroyed by a large fire at the Moncton ICR Shops. But the shops are rebuilt as Moncton maintains its position as ICR headquarters and repair centre for another two decades.

1908 As Canada's Winter Port, Saint John is Canada's second busiest port behind Montreal.

1910 The International Railway Company opens a line measuring 110 miles from Campbellton to meet the NTR and CPR lines at St. Leonard. Four year later, the federal government purchases the line.

1912 The National Transcontinental Railway, Canada's third transcontinental railway, opens.

1913 A new Union Station, built and shared by Canadian National and Canadian Pacific, opens in Saint John. The same year, Alexander Boss Gibson, one of New Brunswick's great railway builders, dies at Marysville. The same year, CP completes the New Brunswick Central Railway into Fredericton, assuming control over a number of long-term leases in central New Brunswick including the Southampton Railway between Millville and Southampton.

1914 The Saint John and Quebec Railway complete the 120 miles of tracks between Westfield along the St. John River Valley to Centreville. Yet the champion of the valley railway, Premier J. Kidd Flemming, is found guilty of political extortion. Construction beyond Centreville is suspended. The same year, the most violence union confrontation in New Brunswick's history occurs as a dispute between the St. John Railway Company and its workers erupted into a bloody riot. Also in 1914, the Dominion government purchases the Cape Tormentine Branch Railway.

1915 The Grand Trunk Railway refuses to accept the operating lease to run National Transcontinental Railway and the Canadian Northern Railway teeters on bankruptcy. The federal government attempts to solve its' "railway problem" by forming the Canadian Government Railways to operate the failing rail lines.

1917 Prince Edward Island's year-round ferry link to the mainland is moved from Pointe-du-Chêne to the shorter connection at Cape Tormentine. The same year, the ICR, the NTR, the Prince Edward Island Railway, Canadian Northern, as well as numerous branches lines become part of the newly created Canadian Government Railways. National railway headquarters are now located in Montreal with ICR maintaining regional headquarters in Moncton.

1918 The Canadian Government Railways becomes the Canadian National Railway and continues to gobble up regional lines and branch railways throughout Canada. Five more branch lines are taken over in New Brunswick including the Albert Railway, the Elgin, Petitcodiac, and Havelock Railway, the St. Martins Railway, the Moncton and Bouctouche Railway, and the York and Carleton Railway.

1920 Placed into bankruptcy, the Grand Trunk Railway becomes part of the Canadian National Railway.

1921 A new railway bridge over the Reversing Falls at Saint John north of the original bridge opens for traffic. The bridge is still in operation today.

1922 CNR's first President, Sir Henry Thornton, is appointed with a promise that politics will no longer play a major role in the operations of Canada's public railway system. Thornton introduces a number of innovative services including a radio network that eventually blossoms into the Canadian Broadcasting Corporation.

1923 With the troubled Grand Trunk Railway folded into Canadian National, Canada now has only two major rail systems.

1925 The first electric diesel locomotive comes into service in Canada and for the next thirty-five years, both steam and diesel locomotives hauled cargo and passengers in Canada.

1927 With high freight rates hurting east coast business, the Dominion passes the Maritime Freight Rate Act, agreeing to pay 20% of all traffic rates that originates or terminates in the region. The same year, Canadian National announces the *Acadian*, a new all-sleeper summer passenger service between Montreal and Halifax. A victim of the Depression, the *Acadian* is cancelled four years later. As well, CNR's "Mastodons of the rails" the Northern locomotive (4-8-4 wheel arrangement) comes on steam with the capacity to haul 150 heavy freight cars the 841 miles from Montreal to Halifax without changing engines.

1929 CNR purchases the Northern Kent Railway Company for $60,000 and continues to operate the branch railway between Richibucto and Kent Junction until 1989.

1936 Fredericton's first railway bridge is destroyed in the great St. John River spring flood.

1941 With literally hundreds of ships steaming into wartime Halifax, each requiring between 500 to 700 boxcars of supplies, and massive amounts of Cape Breton coal on the rails, a bottleneck takes place on CN's single track between Moncton and Truro. To help alleviate congestion, Moncton's CN yard is expanded to handle an additional 2000 cars.

1943 Canadian National Railway has its' most profitable year to date despite paying out wages to over 100,000 workers.

1945 Never fully committed to the Atlantic region, Canadian Pacific sells their New Brunswick Railway land holdings to K.C. Irving. The land was originally acquired from the province in the 1870s as a cash-substitute subsidy for building the railway from Fredericton to Edmundston. CP retains operating rights to the trackage while J.D. Irving acquires some of the province's most valuable timber acreage.

1949 Gulf, Mobile & Ohio becomes the first major US railroad to vanquish all their steam locomotives in favour of the more cost effective diesel engines. The same year, CN acquires the Temiscouata Railway in north-western New Brunswick.

1950 Diesel electric locomotives are introduced in Canada.

1952 Canadian Pacific becomes the first railway in North America to launch the intermodal rail system known as piggybacking, truck trailers on flat cars.

1954 The first passenger train in CN's vast fleet to convert to diesel is the *Ocean Limited*, between Montreal and Halifax.

1957 With passenger levels falling and freight moving to trucks, Canadian National Railway institutes the largest cutback in railway history—11,000 jobs are eliminated while CPR initiates a similar round of layoffs.

1959 With the opening of the St. Lawrence Seaway year-round, Montreal is no longer closed to winter shipping and Saint John loses its preferred status as CPR's Winter Port on the Atlantic.

1960 CP's maintenance of steam engines on its Montreal to Saint John line comes to an end. The steam age in Canada's railway history officially comes to an end as CN steam engine No. 6043 ends her regular run as she pulled into Winnipeg and rolls under a banner that read: "Farewell to 6043 C.N.R.'s Last Steam Locomotive. The same year, Norfolk & Western becomes the last major US railroad to abandon steam for diesel engines. Despite another round of cutbacks, CN still employs 101,000 people down by 30,000 since 1952 but still the largest employer in Canada. And Canadian Pacific has 61,000 employees. In Moncton, the new 830-acre Gordon Yard off Edinburgh Drive opens. The Moncton "hump yard" is CN's first automated hump yard—President Donald Gordon described it best: "the freight car goes over the hump and rolls down to kiss and couple."

1965 CN abandons the Moncton and Bouctouche Railway.

1967 NB Power erects the Mactaquac Dam and the resultant flooding puts an end to the old Valley Railway line between Fredericton and Woodstock.

1971 The US federal government creates Amtrak, essentially nationalizing American train passenger service.

1973 CN and CP passenger service is handed over to the Canadian government agency VIA. Now like the US, passenger service is largely a government responsibility in Canada.

1988 CP establishes a new east coast business enterprise called Canadian Atlantic Railway. With declining traffic over the next five years, CP begins the process of abandoning rail service in eastern Canada.

1989 CN officially abandons the Cape Tormentine Branch Railway as well as all rail lines on Prince Edward Island.

1994 Canadian Pacific ends railway service in Saint John. As CP retreats from the Maritimes, the Irving interests acquire much of the CP trackage in New Brunswick including the 84-mile trunk line from Saint John to St. Croix near McAdam. The New Brunswick Southern Railway becomes owner and operators of the old Western Extension Railway that served as CP's main line in and out of New Brunswick for over one hundred years. New Brunswick Southern Railway also acquires the old St. Stephen Branch Railway that extends 31 miles from St. Stephen to McAdam. A NBSR subsidiary, the Eastern Maine Railway, becomes the operator of the Maine portion of the old Western extension line from Vanceboro 105 miles to Brownville Junction.

1995 Its official as Paul Martin Jr. announces in the House of Commons that Canadian National Railway is being privatized. Canada's vast government created railway, born with Confederation, becomes a publicly traded company with operational headquarters in Chicago.

2002 The New Brunswick Southern Railway becomes the operator of CN's Saint John rail yard.

Sources

Cinders and Saltwater, Shirley Woods, Nimbus Publishing, 1992

Fredericton Flashback, Ted Jones, Nimbus Publishing, 2003

Fredericton & its People, Ted & Anita Jones, Nimbus Publishing, 2002

Historic St. Andrews, Ronald Rees, Nimbus Publishing, 2001

Historic St. Croix, Ronald Rees, Nimbus Publishing, 2003

Historic Fredericton North, Ted & Anita Jones, Nimbus Publishing, 2007

Historic Sussex, Elaine Ingalls Hogg, Nimbus Publishing, 2010

McCully's New Brunswick, Dan Soucoup, Dundurn Press, 2005

No Hay Fever and a Railway, Willa Walker, Goose Lane Editions, 1989

Old Railway Stations of the Maritimes, Peter M. Latta, St Agnes Press, 1998

Ole Larsen's Miramichi, Michael Nowlan, Nimbus Publishing, 1999

The People's Railway, Donald MacKay, Douglas & McIntyre, 1992

The Port of Saint John, Elizabeth McGahan, National Harbours Board, 1982

Railways of New Brunswick, David Nason, New Ireland Press, 1992

Saint John Homeport, Harold Wright & Deborah Stilwell, 2002

Saint John West and Its Neighbours, David Goss and Fred Miller, Arcadia
    Publishing, 1995

PHOTO CREDITS

CHAPTER 5 — ICR BRANCH LINES

CHAPTER 6 — CANADIAN NATIONAL

CHAPTER 12 — NATIONAL TRANSCONTINENTAL RAILWAY & THE VALLEY LINE